MW01193215

Smart Contract Development with Solidity and Ethereum

Building Smart Contracts with the Azure Blockchain

by
Akhil Mittal

FIRST EDITION 2020

Copyright © BPB Publications, India

ISBN: 978-93-88511-919

All Rights Reserved. No part of this publication may be reproduced or distributed in any form or by any means or stored in a database or retrieval system, without the prior written permission of the publisher with the exception to the program listings which may be entered, stored and executed in a computer system, but they can not be reproduced by the means of publication.

LIMITS OF LIABILITY AND DISCLAIMER OF WARRANTY

The information contained in this book is true to correct and the best of author's & publisher's knowledge. The author has made every effort to ensure the accuracy of these publications, but cannot be held responsible for any loss or damage arising from any information in this book.

All trademarks referred to in the book are acknowledged as properties of their respective owners.

Distributors:

BPB PUBLICATIONS
20, Ansari Road, Darya Ganj
New Delhi-110002
Ph: 23254990/23254991

DECCAN AGENCIES
4-3-329, Bank Street,
Hyderabad-500195
Ph: 24756967/24756400

MICRO MEDIA
Shop No. 5, Mahendra Chambers,
150 DN Rd. Next to Capital Cinema,
V.T. (C.S.T.) Station, MUMBAI-400 001
Ph: 22078296/22078297

BPB BOOK CENTRE
376 Old Lajpat Rai Market,
Delhi-110006
Ph: 23861747

Published by Manish Jain for BPB Publications, 20 Ansari Road, Darya Ganj, New Delhi-110002 and Printed at Repro India Ltd, Mumbai

Dedicated to

The book is dedicated to my beloved mother,
Mrs. Rani Mittal

About the Author

Akhil Mittal lives in Noida, India. He is two times Microsoft MVP (Most Valuable Professional) firstly awarded in 2016 continued in 2017 in Visual Studio and Technologies category, C# Corner MVP since 2013, Code Project MVP since 2014, a blogger, author and likes to write/read technical articles, blogs, and books. Akhil actively contributes his technical articles on CodeTeddy (www.codeteddy. com)

He works as a Sr. Consultant with Magic EdTech (www.magiced tech.com) which is recognized as a global leader in delivering end to end learning solutions.

He has an experience of more than 12 years in developing, designing, architecting enterprises level applications primarily in Microsoft Technologies. He has diverse experience in working on cutting edge technologies that include Microsoft Stack, AI, Machine Learning, Blockchain and Cloud computing. Akhil is an MCP (Microsoft Certified Professional) in Web Applications and Dot Net Framework.

Akhil has written few eBooks books on C#, Entity Framework, Web API development and OOP concepts which are published at Amazon Kindle and Leanpub. He has also written a book on Getting started with Chatbots, which is published with BPB publication.

Acknowledgement

No task is a single man's effort. Cooperation and Coordination of various peoples at different levels go into the successful implementation of this book.

There is always a sense of gratitude, which everyone expresses to the others for the help they render during difficult phases of life and to achieve the goal already set. It is impossible to thank individually but I am hereby making a humble effort to thank and acknowledge some of them.

My gratitude to the entire BPB Publications team for the opportunity to work with them on this project.

I would also like to thank my family members, my readers for providing all the encouragement and motivation.

Finally, I want to thank everyone who has directly or indirectly contributed to complete this authentic piece of work.

It is said, **"To err is human, to forgive is divine"**. In this light, the author wishes that the shortcomings of the book will be forgiven. At the same time, the author is open to any kind of constructive criticisms, feedback, corrections, and suggestions for further improvement. All intelligent suggestions are welcome, and the author will try his best to incorporate such invaluable suggestions in the subsequent editions of this book.

Preface

Most people have a bank account, and a bank is a centralized institution that you trust to handle your money and transactions. You may be thinking, what's the big deal? I've been with my bank for years and not had any problems. But that's not really the issue. The thing we're talking about here is that as an individual we are putting a lot of trust into one organization to manage our money. This is also a huge burden for the bank in question. They must keep your data safe and secure to help maintain that trust. Because you are putting your trust into one organization, what is stopping them from accidentally losing some of your money due to systems errors or fraud? These are all threats that the banking system must deal with, and as consumers, we trust them to get it right. But they don't always get it right and things can go wrong. If we take this concept to a higher level than just banks and look at traditional fiat currencies, like the U. S. dollar, Euro, or British pound, these again are very centralized concepts, as they are controlled and regulated by governments. Plus, we are used to centralized control from governments. There is another option, and that is to be decentralized.

One of the benefits of blockchain technology is to get trust on the internet by using decentralization. What do we mean by this?

If you have heard about Bitcoins, you would not have missed gearing about Blockchain as well. The technology behind Bitcoins is Blockchain, but what exactly Blockchain provides?

Imagine if there were an infrastructure where everyone could securely process transactional code and access the data that can never be tampered with. All the transactions are stored in the form of a block which is very hard to manipulate or tamper with, once they are stored on a blockchain. This is the behavior of blockchain where you can store the data in the most trustworthy way in scenarios where there is no trust. Blockchain obviously is not a place where you can store a large amount of data for every transaction. For example, you cannot store a lot of images or documents in bulk, but you can for sure store information that can validate whether your documents or images are tampered with or not.

Most data stored on a blockchain is focused on transactions and states of objects, rather than the actual objects themselves.

This book teaches the concept of Blockchain in detail and gives hands-on experience in developing and deploying Ethereum Blockchain on Azure and Developing Smart Contracts.

This book promises to be a very good starting point for complete novice learners and is quite an asset to advanced readers too. The author has written the book so that the beginners will learn the concepts related to blockchain and smart contract development.

We have developed **4 sections** where you can find the following topics:

Section 1: An introduction to Blockchain and how does it work. The section is divided into 2 chapters to cover the topics.

You will know the concept of Blockchain, the terminology, how blockchain works internally and the cryptographic principles on which blockchain works.

Section 2 This section is named as "Ethereum and DApps". In this section, we'll discuss what Ethereum is and what is its need? We'll look at the execution and funding model of Ethereum. The section will also focus on distributed apps. The section is divided into 2 chapters where chapter one focuses on denominations, Dao, Payment model and transactions and chapter two is more of a hands-on exercise to set-up Ethereum Blockchain on Azure.

Section 3 This section is focused on smart contracts development. The section is divided into 2 chapters where chapter one focuses on setting up the development environment for smart contracts before we start the development and chapter 2 is programming the smart contract which explains the building blocks of smart contract development, getting hands-on with smart contract development, explains smart contract deployment, explains how to test a smart contract. In this section you'll also learn the basics of Solidity language.

Section 4: Explains the usage of blockchain in real world. This section explains what blockchain offers in the day to day life and what are its usages and advantages in the real-world scenario. The section also covers the impact areas of blockchain in education industry.

Errata

We take immense pride in our work at BPB Publications and follow best practices to ensure the accuracy of our content to provide with an indulging reading experience to our subscribers. Our readers are our mirrors, and we use their inputs to reflect and improve upon human errors if any, occurred during the publishing processes involved. To let us maintain the quality and help us reach out to any readers who might be having difficulties due to any unforeseen errors, please write to us at :

errata@bpbonline.com

Your support, suggestions and feedbacks are highly appreciated by the BPB Publications' Family.

Table of Contents

Section - I
What is Blockchain and How does it Work?

The following is the description from MSDN blogs:

At the most basic level of understanding, blockchains are a simple approach to a distributed database. It is a peer-to-peer system with no central authority managing data flow. One of the key ways of removing central control while maintaining data integrity is to have a large distributed network of independent users. You can think of blockchains as distributed databases that a group of individuals controls and that store and share information. The most popular form of a blockchain implementation out there is **Bitcoin**, *which is a cryptocurrency.*

A blockchain is a data structure that makes it possible to create a digital ledger of data and share it among a network of independent parties. There are three main categories of blockchains: public, private (permissioned), and consortium. Each type uses cryptography to allow each participant on any given network to manage the ledger securely without the need for a central authority to enforce the rules. The removal of central authority from database structure is one of the most important and influential aspects of blockchains.

Think of it as a sizeable worldwide computer where everyone can securely access data and execute transactional code. All transactions are stored in blocks of data. These blocks are made in a way that makes them very hard to manipulate or fake once they are stored in the blockchain. Due to the nature of blockchain, you can say that it gives you a reliable way to store data in scenarios where there is no trust. This could be monetary transactions between strangers on the Internet or the ability to securely store your medical information in a way that can only be accessed by those you allow. It is also worth mentioning that blockchain is generally not a place to store large amounts of data for each transaction. You would, for example, generally not store images on a blockchain, but you might store information to validate if an image is being tampered with or not. Most data stored on the blockchain is focused on transactions and states of objects, rather than the actual objects themselves.

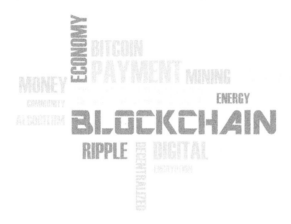

Figure 1.0.1

CHAPTER 1

Blockchain– The Concept, The Genesis

The legacy and drawbacks

It was made very easy to transfer/share audio files using `Napster` (a network for file sharing in **1999**). Since it used a centralized directory network, it was called a mixed peer to peer network. Users using this infrastructure had the flexibility to retain a copy of the file shared. So a single-digit asset retention led to an infinite number of copies being stored on a global network.

In early 2008, millions of credit card numbers were exposed by a known payment system due to data leak, which resulted in fraudulent transactions. These episodes describe the immediate danger of living in the digital world that relies on some mediator who generated money from the transactions and exposed the people to digital exploitation, fraud, and greed.

There was a challenging need to create a digital infrastructure that is mediator free and available to transfer digital assets freely and reliably. The infrastructure demanded to be secure, and the transfer should be peer to peer rather than shared or copied, so it could be trusted and should not have any central governing authority.

Structure

In this chapter, we will discuss the following topics:

- The origin of blockchain.
- Basic blockchain concepts and terminology.
- Characteristics of blockchain.
- Data security aspect.
- How blockchain works.

Objectives

After studying this unit, you should be able to:

- Understand the basics of blockchain and Bitcoin
- Role of security in blockchain.
- Concept of transactions and internal working of blockchain

The Bitcoin blockchain - Genesis

On January 3, 2009, about 50 digital coins were mined via a new kind of infrastructure that not only mined but also recorded the coins on a public ledger that was impossible to tamper with and was replicated on a decentralized peer to peer network on the Internet. Those 50 digital coins were named as bitcoins and were registered as the genesis block, that is, the first establishment to be called **Bitcoin blockchain**. The one crucial thing that makes this infrastructure unique is that cryptocurrency powered by blockchain has no centralized governance and trust authority like banks and other financial institutions to validate the transactions. The blockchains do not depend on a mediator; this makes it possible to transfer digital assets globally on the Internet with no involvement of a middleman.

The terminology blockchain is not only limited to bitcoins but applies to all cryptocurrencies in general. The data located in the blockchain is encrypted with modern cryptographic techniques, which makes it more reliable and tamper-proof. It is not prone to any single point of failure as it is replicated on each node that consists of the peer-to-peer network, which makes the technology more trustworthy and available.

Bitcoin technology keeps on maturing rapidly since its launch, and hence there is a drastic variation of their implementation details, making the study of blockchains vast, complex, and dynamic. Since the genesis, blockchains have become more mature to work smarter and faster. It is being perfected and refined more and more as it expands. Some blockchains like `Ethereum` also support smart contracts, that is, allowing scripting on the blockchain. And so, you can apply your customized constraints over the blockchain nodes. So, beyond the limitations, blockchain technology has proved to be a new kind of hack-proof, programmable storage technology.

Concepts - Bitcoin

Before we start to dig into the details, we must spend some time on the origin of the technology. You might already have heard about the emerging currency called Bitcoins. Bitcoin is the first broadly used cryptocurrency. A cryptocurrency is something that only exists as a digital currency. It does not hold any underlying value. It is not something you can withdraw from the bank and hold in your hand. It is only a unique string of letters and numbers attached to an ulnar.

Bitcoin is a form of digital currency that is created and held entirely electronically instead of being printed currency. Unlike banks and traditional fare currencies, no one controls or runs Bitcoin. The Bitcoin algorithms control the rate at which new Bitcoins are introduced, and people are incentivized to help maintain and mine new coins by being paid themselves in Bitcoin. It is a first in a new category of currencies called cryptocurrencies. It can be spent electronically for both digital and physical goods. There are even vending machines that will let you purchase goods by using your mobile phone to pay for products with the Bitcoin that you own. But the essential feature of Bitcoin is that it is entirely decentralized. No one company or government owns or has any control over Bitcoin.

After the gold standard was eliminated in the U. S. in 1971, this is true for the U. S. dollar as well. You have a balance at your bank account, and you trust them to make sure that they keep a secure ledger over incoming and outgoing values. Banks are part of a vast global network where transactions can be done between banks, and currency can be exchanged. With Bitcoins, there is no central system. There is no bank, and there is no way to revert transactions once they are done. All transactions are transparent and can be entirely anonymous. Bitcoins could not have existed without the blockchain, and Bitcoins is its first broad use.

Blockchain

So, we have just introduced the term blockchain while discussing Bitcoin. Blockchain has often been talked about as the next revolution in computing, and it's redefining how we interact and transact on the Internet. This may sound very theatrical, but as we discuss what a blockchain is and where it can be used, you'll start to see why these claims make sense.

The notion of a cryptographically secured chain of blocks was described by *Stuart Haber* and *Scott Stornetta* already in 1991. The first recognized work on the decentralized digital currency on using similar technology was done by *Nick Szabo* in *1998*. But it took almost 10 years until the blockchain concept was getting mature and published by *Satoshi Nakamoto* in *2008*. *Satoshi* is by most considered to be the founder of Bitcoin in 2009. However, it is worth mentioning that, as of now, no one knows who *Satoshi Nakamoto* is. It is highly likely that *Satoshi* is not a real person and that it is a pseudonym used by someone else. There are many interesting theories around who it is, and this adds to the mystic and enchantment of Bitcoin and the underlying technology. Race forward to *2014* and the blockchain is hitting a mainstream term used by financial and technical media. Large companies are picking up speed on blockchain development. There's massive investment being done by traditional legacy software companies like IBM and Microsoft. Still, there is also a large and rapidly growing mass of start-up companies getting their blockchain implementations out to the market.

Characteristics of blockchain

Let's look at the characteristics of blockchain. First, it is a global singleton. If you know how singletons work for a program, you can think of the blockchain objects as global singleton instances. The blockchain is natively object-oriented, where code and data reside together. However, objects are securely separated from each other. It's unstoppable. There is no one in control over a blockchain. It cannot be stopped, and it cannot have a central failure. No government or corporation can censor it, and it's very resistant to being hacked. There is no power cord to pull nor a single point of attack. Blockchain, by its nature, is accessible. Everywhere there's the Internet, and you can access the blockchain by using a large number of clients and technologies. And most of all, it's verifiable. Everyone that has access to the blockchain can verify every single transaction from the beginning of time. This enables everyone to audit everything, and as we will learn in the next couple of sections, it is quite easy to do so.

In short, blockchain is a kind of data structure that is tamper-proof and can track the digital assets as they pass from owner to owner. The digital asset could be a digital coin like Bitcoin, any document, or the transaction could be a monetary transaction between strangers on the Internet. It can, for example, give you an ability to store your medical information where only you have secure access or someone you allow would have that access. Not only this, but an asset with a digital fingerprint can also be tracked on a blockchain.

Blockchain makes sure that the ownership of digital assets should be transferred rather than being shared or copied and so it solves the problem related to *double-spending.* Blockchain accomplishes this outstanding coup rapidly and internationally with no central authority to govern. This makes commerce more advanced for businesses, thereby eliminating the middleman and transactional fees.

Hashing

The core of any blockchain resides in the concept of hashing. Hashing is basically to execute a mathematical algorithm that creates a result with a given length regardless of the input given. The result of a hashing function is called a **hash**, and you can think of them as digital fingerprints. Hashing is a one-way function, meaning the function will always return the same result given the same input, but you can never regenerate the input based on the result of the hashing algorithm. As a simple example. Let's say that we have a straightforward hashing algorithm that takes any number between 0 and 45 as input. The algorithm then doubles the number and rounds to the nearest 10. This means that if input 5, you will get a hashing result of 10. The same will be true if you input 3 or 4, but if you input 9, the hash will 20 instead. The length of the result will always be two digits, even if you give a single digit input. If you run the algorithm several times using the same input, you'll always get the same result, but you would not be able to figure out what the input was.

When hashing in real life, a much more advanced hashing algorithm is, of course, used. The most used hashing algorithms are generally well known and available to the public. Hashing algorithms are generally created to execute fast. The more advanced you want your algorithms to be, the more power it takes to execute. A ubiquitous hashing algorithm used with blockchain is the **SHA   256**. It is one of several checksum hashing algorithms, and it will produce a long text string as a result. It's designed by the *American National Security Agency,* and it's made available to the public. The SHA is a family of hashing algorithms. The number following the names lets you know the complexity of the implementation.

Widespread use for hashing is when storing passwords in a database. If you store the password in clear text in your database, your usage might be at risk if your database is hacked and the hacker gets access to the database table with usernames and passwords; however, if the password is hashed, the hacker will have a tough time figuring out the passwords. They will then need to compare the passwords with known hashed results where the input is known less well. This can be done by generating a large number of hashes based on random text strings or even by pre-existing lists of common hashes. The longer a password is, the less likely it is that the hacker can find the input that created a particular hash and still if they were able to figure it out, they wouldn't be 100% sure so they would have to test every combination that led to the same hash. Because hash algorithms always give the same result given the same input and always give a fixed length of the result, they are also ideal for verifying the consistency of more massive amounts of data. If you put the entire *Wikipedia* website through a hashing algorithm and save the resulting hash, you could quickly figure out if someone has changed anything on the website. Even a single comma would result in a different hash result. So, when comparing two hashes, it is rapid to determine if they match or not. If they match, nothing has changed. If they do not match, someone has altered the original. This is a very sure and quick way to figure out if the data has been compromised. And another benefit is that you do not need to store the original data to see if anything has changed. All you need to store is the initial hash. Hashing algorithms are also used in many areas of modern security, where the need for consistency is high. For example, in secure communication where timestamps are exchanged. While we are discussing hashing, let's quickly talk about a related topic called a **Merkle tree.**

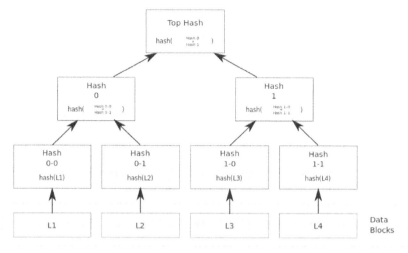

Image source: https://commons.wikimedia.org/wiki/File:Hash_Tree.svg

Figure 1.1.1

A Merkle tree is a hash of hashes, which makes it quick and somewhat easy to confirm large amounts of data and transactions. Let's say we have four sets of data. To simplify, I'm using one word here for each data block, but this could easily be, for example, transactions in real life. These words produce four different hashes. In the Merkle tree, groups of these hashes are hashed together to create a hash of hashes. These hashes are then hashed together as well, creating what we call a root or top hash. To figure out if something has changed anywhere in the Merkle tree, we only need to see if the root hash has changed, and you can then follow the tree down to see where the change is done.

Block

Now that we have some basic terminology covered, let's begin to look at the actual block in the blockchain. A block consists of data and its resulting hash. If we go ahead and change any data in the block, the hash will change, and the block will be invalid. It also includes the nonce, which is input to the hashing algorithm that would result in the first part of the hash to be something predefined like a set of zeros. It's not possible to predict the nonce so that it can be considered as proof of work by the machine creating the hash. Let's say that we require our hash to have a leading number of four zeros. Whenever we change anything, we will need to rerun the hashing algorithm until we figure out which nouns to set. This is called **mining the block.**

Let's see what happens when we have a chain of blocks. When we are looking at the chain, the block also contains a block number, meaning which order it has in the blockchain. A block also must contain a timestamp, but most importantly, the block in a blockchain will include the hash of the previous block. This means that if you alter any of the value in one of the blocks, you will break all the blocks following in the chain. This is also where the Merkle tree, mentioned earlier, is used. The only way to fix the blockchain will then be to mine all the blocks after the changed block and make the nonce hashes all over. In the blockchain, we distribute a chain of blocks to a vast number of computers. This means that the chain exists in multiple locations. Depending on the implementation of blockchain you are using, it could be millions of replications of the chain. This means that we could quickly figure out if something has changed, even if one of the chains has been re-mined. The resulting hashes would be different from one chain and blockchain works in a way where the chain that has the most work put into it wins, so to say. The altered chain would then be rejected by the distributed blockchain and be removed. To better understand why it's so hard to fake anything in a blockchain, let's talk a little bit about the concept of forks.

Forks

First, we have our user, *Kent*. He has a balance of 100 Bitcoins, and he wants to buy a new *Tesla car*. He got the Bitcoins from his very rich, but still, down-to-earth mother called *Sharon*. He finds a vendor that is selling cars using Bitcoins. He adds the transaction to the blockchain and drives away, smiling in his electric wonder machine, but when he comes back, he sees a *Mercedes* that he likes on the Internet. The vendor also accepts Bitcoins. Unfortunately, he is now breaking, but he kept information about his previously owned Bitcoins. He, therefore, tries to add a block to the blockchain where he spends the same money once more. This creates a fork in the blockchain, and for him to fix it, he must have a lot of computing power at his hands. Since the blockchain consists of having to prove that you put work into the calculations, he would have to have almost the same computing resources as the rest of the blockchain for his new chain to be accepted. This is quite unlikely, but we have seen some people trying to do this, but this fork has always been downloaded and removed. Since it requires so much computing power to do this, it's an excellent incentive to stay honest. The same computing power could have been used to mine blocks legally instead.

Public versus private

Now that we have investigated blockchain as a general term let's start to consider the implementations of it. First, blockchains can be either public or private. In a public blockchain, everyone with an Internet connection can connect to the chain. The way the public chains are funded is that you generally need to pay for storage, transaction, and execution costs to the entities that have joined the chain. This can be quite expensive. Just imagine the Bitcoin going from only being worth a couple of cents to over $1000 only a few years later. You might regret paying 1% of a Bitcoin for your transactions back in 2013; however, as soon as the different currencies that are being used stabilize, this will be less of a problem. Since the public blockchains are generally widely distributed, there's also no given point for attack for a hacker. They cannot target a single datacentre or company to bring down the chain. But this depends on how well the chain is supported by the community. As soon as the community support is gone, the chain is also gone. This raises a lot of questions and concerns that we don't have any right answers to yet, but I'm sure that over the next couple of years, we'll get more research and a better understanding of how these communities work. One of the most significant benefits and a challenge of a public blockchain in a business context is that it is democratic. The community must decide how, for example, forks are being handled, and generally, your stake in the chain controls how many volts you have. When looking at private blockchain, many consider these not to be real blockchains as they are not truly distributed and democratic.

With a private blockchain, you are closer to a traditional database. Some people call private blockchains for shared distributed databases. Since you will own the infrastructure, you can also control the cost and financing of the chain. This might be both a benefit and a challenge depending on the company goals you have. You're also dealing with known entities, and you are in control of who can access your chain. For a lot of companies dealing with sensitive data, it's required by law in many countries that the data is stored in a specific area. Since we have much more control with a private blockchain, it can be an excellent way for companies to transition to the technology, while legislation and usage patterns evolve. You are, however, losing out on a few critical areas, and there are also fewer points of attack, so your private blockchain might be easier to take down than a public and highly distributed implementation.

Blockchain - Behind the scenes

So how does it all work? It begins with someone doing a single or a group of transactions. A transaction is typically sending data in the form of a contract. Depending on the blockchain implementation you are using, it can also involve cryptocurrency being sent from one account to another. The transactions are sent to an extensive peer-to-peer network of computers. These are generally distributed all over the world. Each computer is called a node, and they all have a copy of the existing data. Then the transaction is executed and validated based on pre-shared contracts and scripts. This ensures that all nodes execute using the same set of rules. When the transaction has executed, the result is added to the blockchain. Since this is done at each node, you would have to compromise every node in the chain to compromise the transaction.

When doing transactions in the blockchain, some aspects are necessary for it to have the characteristics previously mentioned. First, all transactions are atomic. This means that the full operation run or nothing at all. Let's say you have a monetary transaction. You would want to ensure that both the function that credits one account and a function that debits another are executed successfully. If one of them fails, the entire transaction should fail. If not, you might end up either destroying or creating money. However, unfortunately, even with blockchain, there's nothing that prevents you from writing harmful code, so you still need to ensure that you execute transactions in the right order. Secondly, transactions run independently of each other. So, no two operations can interact or interfere with each other. It must be inspectable. Every single method call that comes to blockchain comes with the actual address to the caller.

Just think about it. This gives a unique possibility for securing and auditing solutions on a very, very wide scale. This is unique to blockchain. At least I'm not aware of anywhere else you can do this. Blockchain objects are immortal. That means that all data from an object are permanent. The code for an object can never be changed, and you can never delete an object externally. The only way to remove an object from the blockchain is that if it is programmed to remove itself. So, think about it. When writing code for the blockchain, you, really, really need to make sure that this is what you want to do. Because you never alter or remove it.

Transactions and blocks

At the center of the blockchain, we have a record of transactions, much like a traditional accounting ledger. These transactions could be a movement of money between people or companies, or it could be any piece of information that is transactional, like the transferring of property deeds or the tracking of movement of inventory between different companies. Data stored in a blockchain is designed to be kept in a way that makes it virtually impossible to change the data once it is in the blockchain without being detected by other users. As we discussed earlier, traditional banking transactions are verified by a central bank or authority. Blockchain applications could replace these more centralized systems with these centralized ones where verification comes from the consensus of multiple users participating in the blockchain.

A blockchain must do two main things. It needs to gather data or transactions together and put them in blocks. Then those block needs to be chained together securely using cryptography. When the transactions are put onto the block, we use cryptographic hashing or digital fingerprinting to link the transactions together. This means that if any part of the transaction changes, the entire block will fail verification, which will flag it to the other users. At the top of the block, we have a hash that represents all the transactions in that block. Let's call this the block address. It's these block addresses that we use to chain the blocks together because each block knows who his previous block address is, which is how we form the chain.

For a block to be entered in the chain, the person creating the block must solve a complex mathematical puzzle when calculating the block address. This is called mining the block with proof-of-work. The puzzle was designed to be computationally expensive and must happen before each block in the chain. Let's say this problem takes 10 minutes to calculate. Now imagine we have 1000 blocks in our chain. So, the total time spent calculating all the block addresses is 166 hours. Now imagine someone wants to overwrite the data in the first block. They must recalculate that block's mining puzzle, which takes 10 minutes. But because all the other blocks are cryptographically linked, if you change a block, then you need to recalculate the hashes and addresses for the next block and so on and so on. So, to change data in block 1 means that you need to spend 166 hours or nearly 7 days recalculating the whole chain. Just imagine how long we are talking if the chain is long and the puzzle takes longer than 10 minutes. The longer the chain, the more secure it is. When these blocks are added to the chain, a copy is sent to everyone participating in the network. This is how we establish trust because so many people have a copy. Let's say 100 people have copies of the whole chain, and someone tries to change one of the blocks. They might add this into their chain, but there will 99 other people who do not agree with their change. Now don't worry too much if you don't completely understand all this now. We are going to explore this in much more detail in upcoming chapters.

Securing your data

Data stored in the blockchain is generally available to everyone that has access to the chain. This gives some challenges, but it will also lead you to think about security first. In some applications, it's no problem that everyone has access to everything, but in most cases, you want to assure that you control who has your data. There are two ways to handle this. The first is **obfuscation**. This means to make the data relevant only to those who know its meaning. One example of this is with Bitcoins. With the address of any account, it's a long string of letters and numbers. No one in the chain knows who the address is physically connected to, and they don't need to know, but everyone knows every transaction going between the different account addresses. It's up to you if you want to be anonymous or not. If you don't share a connection to your account address, there's no way for anyone to know that you are the owner of the account.

Another example of obfuscation is to have the data contain IDs and status codes. Unless you know what the different IDs are connected to, the data is really of no use to you. The problem with relying only on obfuscation is that you always run the risk of someone making the connections due to a breach in the system controlling the keys and connect the data. To deal with this, you can make use of encryption. When you encrypt a message or the transaction payload, you apply a two-way algorithm to the message in a way that can only be decoded if you know a password or a passphrase. This means that the data can be available to everyone, but only those who have the keys to decrypt the message can make sense of it. There are many different encryption algorithms, and as with hashing, they are continuously evolving. The next section of the book will focus on those.

Conclusion

In this chapter, we studied the basics of blockchain and what it is. The section focussed around hashing and why it's essential for understanding how a blockchain works. After that, we started to understand how a block is built and how it is connected to a chain. Security is an especially important aspect to consider, so the basics of obfuscation and encryption were explained to give an idea of what it is all about. The section explained the difference between public and private blockchain implementations.

Now that the basics are clear, we'll raise a bar a bit high and deep dive into security. In the next chapter, we will study about hashing techniques used in blockchain and learn about digital signatures.

Questions

1. What is blockchain?
2. What is the difference between blockchain and Bitcoin?
3. What are blocks and transactions in blockchain?
4. How is blockchain secure?
5. What is hashing?
6. Is blockchain different from banking ledgers?
7. How is a blockchain ledger different from an ordinary one?
8. What type of records can be kept in a blockchain? Is there any restriction on the same?
9. What exactly do you know about the security of a block?
10. Is it possible to modify the data once it is written in a block?

CHAPTER 2
Blockchain – Cryptographic Principles

In this section, we're going to take a closer look at some of the cryptographic primitives you will need to build out a blockchain data structure. We're going to look at hashing, authenticated hashing, and digital signatures. The scope of the book is limited to learning and understanding about blockchain, so this section is not detailed about cryptography, but instead gives an idea of how the cryptography techniques work. Cryptography is a fascinating subject, and a lot could be found over the Internet or in other books dedicated to the topic.

Image source: Pixabay.com
Figure 1.2.1

Structure

In this chapter, we will discuss the following topics:

- Hashing techniques
- HMAC
- Digital signatures

Objectives

After studying this unit, you should be able to:

- Understand what is hashing?
- Understand types of hashing
- Learn about digital signatures and their significance.

Hashing

The process of hashing data is a fundamental technique using cryptography, and it forms a backbone of what we're going to look at regarding building up our blockchain implementation. A cryptographic hash function is an algorithm that takes an arbitrary block of data and returns a fixed-size string, the cryptographic hash value, such that any accidents or intentional change to that data will change the hash value. The data to be encoded is often called the **message**, and the hash value is also sometimes called the **message digest**, or only the digest.

The ideal cryptographic hash function has four main properties. First, it must be easy to compute the hash value for any given message. This means that with any block of data, it should be easy to run a hashing function to calculate the hash. Next, it should be infeasible to generate a message that has a given hash. This means it should be infeasible to generate some original data that will result in a predetermined hash code or digest. Next, it should be infeasible to modify a message without changing the hash. This means if you change just a single bit in the data that you want to hash, then the resulting hash code is entirely different. And finally, it should be infeasible to find two different messages with the same hash. This means you've got two different blocks of data that you want to create a hash code for. They should not both end up with the same final hash code. This is referred to as a **hash collision.**

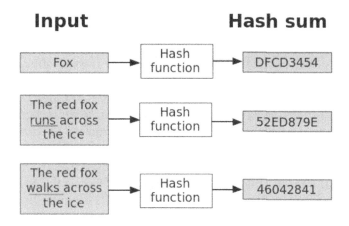

Image source: https://commons.wikimedia.org/wiki/File:Hash_function.svg

Figure 1.2.2

Another way of thinking of a hash function is that of creating a unique fingerprint of a piece of data. Generating a hash digest of a block of data is very easy to do in *C#*. There are various algorithms you can use, such as *MD5, SHA-1, SHA-256*, and *SHA-512*. A hash function is a one-way function. That means that once you've hashed in data, you cannot reverse it back to the original data. On the flip side to this, encryption is designed to be a two-way operation. Once you've encrypted some data using a key, you can then reverse your operation and decrypt the data by using the same key.

Figure 1.2.3

When you're hashing data, the hash will be the same every time you operate, unless the original data changes in some way. Even if the data only changes by one bit, the resulting hash code will be completely different. This makes hashing the perfect mechanism for checking the integrity of data. This is useful when you want to send data across a network to another recipient. Before sending the data, you calculate the hash of the original data to get its unique fingerprints. You then send the data and the hash to the recipient. They then recalculate the hash of the original data they have just received and then compare it to the hash that you sent. If the hash codes are the same, then the data has been successfully received without any data loss or corruption. If the hash codes do not match, then the data received is not the same as the data initially sent, and you shouldn't trust that data. The two most common hashing methods used are *MD5* and the *SHA* family of hashes, *SHA-1, SHA-256,* and *SHA-512. MD5* is generally not used much these days for new software, but it is still relevant if you are integrating with older systems that still use MD5 hashes. For this chapter, we'll focus just on *SHA.*

SHA

The SHA family is a family of cryptographic hash functions published by the *National Institute of Standards and Technologies (NIST).* The SHA family covers some different variants, including SHA-1, which is a 160-bit hash function that resembles the early *MD5* algorithm. This was designed by the *National Security Agency* to be part of the digital signature algorithm. Cryptographic weaknesses were discovered in *SHA-1,* and this standard was no longer approved for most cryptographic uses after *2010.* Next, we have *SHA-2,* which is a family of 2 similar hash functions with different block sizes known as *SHA-256* and *SHA-512.* They differ in word sizes. *SHA-256* uses 32-bit words, whereas SHA-512 uses 64-bit words. These versions of the SHA algorithm were also designed by the National Security Agency. Finally, we have *SHA-3,* which is a hash function formally called **Keccak**, chosen in 2012 after a public competition amongst Non-National Security Agency designers. It supports the same hash lengths as *SHA-2,* and its internal structure differs significantly from the rest of the *SHA* family. Implementing secure hashes into your applications is a very straightforward process.

The *.NET* framework provides cryptography-related functionality encapsulated in `System.Security.Cryptography` namespace and its classes. The `HashAlgorithm` class is the base class for hash algorithms, including *MD5, RIPEMD-160, SHA-1, SHA-256, SHA-384,* and *SHA512.*

The `ComputeHash` method of `HashAlgorithm` computes a hash. It takes a byte array or stream as an input and returns a hash in the form of a byte array of 256 bits.

Following is the code of simple console application in C# showing how to compute SHA hash.

```
using System;
using System.Text;
using System.Security.Cryptography;

namespace Cryptography
{
    class Program
    {
        static void Main(string[] args)
        {
            string input = "Blockchain";
            Console.WriteLine("Raw data: {0}", input);
            string hashedData = ComputeSha256Hash(input);
            Console.WriteLine("Hash {0}", hashedData);
            Console.
WriteLine(ComputeSha256Hash("Blockchain"));
            Console.ReadLine();
        }

        static string ComputeSha256Hash(string rawData)
        {
            // Create a SHA256
            using (SHA256 sha256Hash = SHA256.Create())
            {
                // ComputeHash - returns byte array
                byte[] bytes = sha256Hash.
ComputeHash(Encoding.UTF8.GetBytes(rawData));

                // Convert byte array to a string
```

```
                StringBuilder builder = new
StringBuilder();

                for (int i = 0; i < bytes.Length; i++)

                {

                    builder.Append(bytes[i].
ToString("x2"));

                }

                return builder.ToString();

            }

        }

    }

}
```

The code mentioned above has a `Main()` method, which is the entry point of the console application. The `Main ()` method sets input as a string Blockchain in the variable named input. Then a method is called named `ComputeSha256Hash()`, which is defined below the `Main()` method and is responsible for converting the input string to the hash. The method creates the instance of SHA256 class and calls the method ComputeHash(), accepting a byte array of the input and computes the hash, which is then returned to the caller method, that is, `Main()`. Once the hash is created, the method is called again to check if the hash is again computed the same or is different. And we see the hash is again the same. The following image shows the output.

```
Raw data: Blockchain
Hash 625da44e4eaf58d61cf048d168aa6f5e492dea166d8bb54ec06c30de07db57e1
625da44e4eaf58d61cf048d168aa6f5e492dea166d8bb54ec06c30de07db57e1
```

Figure 1.2.4

Authenticated hashing (HMAC)

There is one step further than we can go with SHA-256 hashing, and that is to create what is called a **hashed message authentication** code. Fundamentally, this is the same as hashing but is taken a step further. If you combine a one-way function such as SHA-256 with a secret cryptographic key, then you get what is called a hash message authentication code, or an **HMAC** for short. Like a hash code, an HMAC is used when you want to verify the integrity of a message. An HMAC also allows you to verify the authentication of that message because only a person who knows the key can calculate the same hash of that message. An HMAC can be used with different hashing functions like *MD5* or the SHA family of algorithms. The cryptographic strength of an HMAC depends on the size of the key that is used. In our case, in this course, we are going to be using an HMAC with a 256-bit or 32-byte key. Hash message authentication codes are used when you need to check both the integrity and the authenticity of a message.

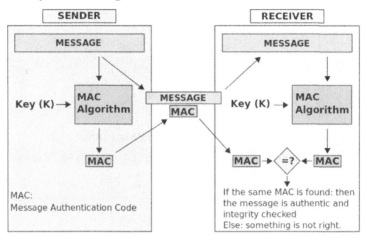

Figure 1.2.5

For example, consider a scenario in which you are sent a piece of data along with its hash. You can verify the integrity of the message by recomputing the hash of that message and comparing it with the original hash that you have received; however, you don't know for sure that the message and the hash were not sent by someone you know or trust. If you used a hashed message authentication code, you could recompute the HMAC by using a secret key that only you and the trusted third party know and compare it with the HMAC you just received. This serves the purpose of authentication.

In the following example, I'll show you how to use an *HMAC* that uses a 32-byte or 256-bit key and the HMAC based on the *SHA-256* hashing algorithm. In addition to the hashed MAC *SHA-256*, you can use *SHA-1, SHA-512,* and *SHA* of *MD5*. The interface is all the same, but for this course, we'll just be using the *SHA-256* variant.

```csharp
using System;
using System.Text;
using System.Security.Cryptography;

namespace Cryptography
{
    class Program
    {
        static void Main(string[] args)
        {
            string input = "Blockchain";
            string key = "SecretKey";

            string hashedData = GetHash(input,key);
            Console.WriteLine("Hash {0}", hashedData);
            Console.ReadLine();
        }

        public static string GetHash(string toBeHashed,
string key)
        {
            var keyToUse = Encoding.UTF8.GetBytes(key);
            var message = Encoding.UTF8.
GetBytes(toBeHashed);
            using(var hmac = new HMACSHA256(keyToUse))
            {
                return Convert.ToBase64String(hmac.
ComputeHash(message));
            }

        }

    }

}
```

In the preceding code, you can see a snippet of code that calculates an SHA-256-based hashed message authentication code. Like the standard *SHA-256* hash, the hashing class deals with byte arrays, but in this example, I've put in the necessary string to byte array conversions to show you what these look like. First, this method takes a string of our data to be hashed and the string representing the key. The key can be anything that you'd like, but it shouldn't be longer than 256 bits or 32 bytes in this case. Next, we use the Encoding. *UTF8*. GetBytes method to convert the data to be hashed and the key strings into byte arrays. Then we create an instance to the hash HMACSHA256 class and pass the byte array of our key into it. Next on the HMAC object, we call `ComputeHash` and pass in the byte array of the message that we want to create the authenticated hash for. The result of this is also a byte array, which we convert back into a `Base64` encoded string using the `Convert`. ToBase64 string method. Now that we have covered hashing and authenticated hashing. Following is the output of the console application when executed.

```
Hash 7geGMPA1/X4v2lj8c22gRKVO/+E9WbBa/1ndijUeYa0=
```

Figure 1.2.6

Digital signatures

An essential function of cryptography is to ensure non-repudiation of a sent message. This is where the receiver of that message cannot deny that the message is authentic. Additional signatures are a technique used to help demonstrate that the message is authentic. A valid digital signature gives the recipient a reason to believe that the message was created by a known sender, such that the sender cannot deny having sent that message. Digital signatures give you both authentication and non-repudiation. Authentication because the signatures had to be created by a user with a valid, private key, and non-repository so that a receiver can trust that the message was signed by a known sender, as only they know the private key. So how do digital signatures do all this? For the receiver of the message, a digital signature allows the receiver to believe that the message was sent by the correct sender. This can be thought of as the digital equivalent to a signature on a letter, except a digital signature is much harder to forge. A digital signature consists of the following three algorithms: the public and private key generation using RSA, a signing algorithm that uses the private key to create the signature, and a signature verification algorithm that uses the public key to test if the message is authentic. The private and public keys are two keys that are mathematically linked. The public key, as the name suggests, can be known by anyone, and the private key should only be known by you, the sender of the message. So, therefore, it's this private key that must be kept secret.

Let's now look at an example of how a digital signature works. In this example, Alice has sent in a message to Bob, and that message will be signed with a digital signature.

Image credit: https://upload.wikimedia.org/wikipedia/commons/ 9/93/Ss_digitalsignature.png

Figure 1.2.7

First, Alice encrypts some data that she wants to send to *Bob*. For this example, it doesn't matter whether the data was encrypted with a symmetric or asymmetric encryption algorithm. Once this data has been encrypted, Alice takes a hash of that data. Next, *Alice* signs the data with her private signing key. This creates a digital signature. Then, *Alice* sends the encrypted data, its hash, and the signature to *Bob*. First, *Bob* recalculates the hash of the encrypted data. *Bob* then verifies the digital signature using the calculated hash and the public signing key. This will tell *Bob* whether the signature is valid or not. If it is valid, *Bob* can be confident and see it was *Alice* that sent him the message in the first place, as it could only have been signed using her private signing key, which only *Alice* knows. If this signature was not valid, then *Bob* should not trust the origin and authenticity of the message. As we just mentioned, the digital signature signing is based on *RSA*. But with *RSA*, we need to encrypt some data. You encrypt the data with the recipient's public key, and then the recipient decrypts it with their private key. With a digital signature, signing and verifying is the other way around. When the sender signs a message, they use their private key, and then the recipient verifies the signature using the sender's public key. It is since we've signed the sender's private key that a recipient can trust that a message was sent by that sender, as it will only be them that knows that private key.

Conclusion

In this chapter, we learned about the security aspects and cryptographic principles. The idea was to get a sense of what cryptography is, how it can be useful in securing transactions and blocks data while developing a blockchain. The technology doesn't matter here. It's the concept that matters. For example, the chapter used *Microsoft DotNet* and *C#* as the technology to show how simple methods could leverage existing libraries to generate hashes or securing the data.

Questions

1. What is hashing, and what are types of hashing?
2. What is authenticated hashing?
3. What are digital signatures?
4. How a block does is recognized in the blockchain approach?
5. What are block identifiers?
6. What exactly do you know about the security of a block?

Section - II
Ethereum
and
DApps

In this section, we'll discuss what Ethereum is and what is its need? We'll look at the execution and funding model of Ethereum.

The section will also focus on distributed apps.

Figure 2.1.1

CHAPTER 1
Distributed Applications

So, what is Ethereum?

Ethereum is one of the largest and most well- established blockchains, and it's based on the proposal from *Vitalik Buterin* in *2013*. It was publicly available in *2015*. Since it is open-source, it's very easy to use it for private blockchains. It is not just a platform, but also programming language running on a blockchain so we can build and publish a distributed application called **distributed applications (DApps).** Ethereum has its cryptocurrency called **Ether** that, in many ways, is like Bitcoins. One benefit of Ethereum is that it has speedy transaction time where the block time is set to a few seconds as compared to minutes for Bitcoin. This can make it more suitable for applications where you need a fast response, for example, checkout payments and rapid workflows.

Another big thing about Ethereum is that it has a method for funding transactions depending on their computational complexity, bandwidth use, and storage needs. This is the difference from the Bitcoin blockchain where transactions compete equally with each other. This means that you can pay to get faster transactions. The proof of work that other blockchains are using has had some negative impact where large computing compasses are solving hard problems just to prove that they put work into it. This is a big waste of resources, and Ethereum is moving more towards proof of stake where they use direct economic stake instead of proof of work. It comes down a few reasons to explore Ethereum that you should also consider when you select the blockchain implementation, you would like to use for your applications. First of all, the Ethereum development community is growing, and it's very easy to find resources and tools for rapid development. With emerging technologies like blockchain, it's essential to consider how well the community is adapting the different implementations, and to be honest, the Ethereum community is awe-inspiring, and it's easy to get help from them. Ethereum has learned quite a bit from the Bitcoin development as well, and it's by many considered to be an evolution of this. It targets application development well with an easy-to-use contract language. Later in this course, we'll be spending two modules working with this. It's also rather easy to set up your private blockchains and test implementations. Ethereum also has a broad commercial adoption, especially at the enterprise level, and it fits well into enterprise solutions and existing architectures.

Ether is the currency that is used with Ethereum. You can use it like any other cryptocurrency, and it's the base for paying for transactions in Ethereum. It's traded under the **eth** symbol, and there are many ways to trade Ether. If you consider investing in Ether, you should understand that this is a very volatile currency, at least for now. Ether has seen some massive ups and downs, and it's not uncommon that it fluctuates more than 20% weekly. You should be very careful about investing, but if you have money to spare, investing in Ether can be an excellent investment over time, or as with any cryptocurrency or new investment possibilities, you could end up losing everything you have invested. Like all currencies, Ether also has denominations to make it easier in daily use.

Structure

In this chapter, we will discuss the following topics:

- Denominations
- DAO
- Payment model-gas
- Transactions

Objectives

After studying this unit, you should be able to:

- Understand about distributed apps.
- Start gas and gas prices
- Transactions.

Denominations

Currently, there are 12 denominations, and they are generally given names inspired by those who have been a significant influence on Ethereum. The currently smallest use denomination is *Wei*, and *1 ETH is 1 quintillion, Wei.*

Finney is also quite often used, and *1 ETH is 1000 Finney.* Szabo has, of course, also gotten its denomination, and *1 ETH is 1 million* Szabo. When denominations get more substantial than *1 ETH,* we use Kether, where the **K** stands for kilo, meaning that that 1K ETH is 1000 ETH. The same with Mether where the **M** stands for mega, Gether meaning Giga ETH, and so on.

Value (in wei)	Exponent	Common Name	SI Name
1	1	wei	wei
1,000	10^3	babbage	kilowei or femtoether
1,000,000	10^6	lovelace	megawei or picoether
1,000,000,000	10^9	shannon	gigawei or nanoether
1,000,000,000,000	10^{12}	szabo	microether or micro
1,000,000,000,000,000	10^{15}	finney	milliether or milli
1,000,000,000,000,000,000	*10^{18}*	*ether*	*ether*
1,000,000,000,000,000,000,000	10^{21}	grand	kiloether
1,000,000,000,000,000,000,000,000	10^{24}		megaether

Figure 2.1.2

When talking about Ether, you should also be aware that there exists something called **Ethereum Classic** that is traded under the symbol ETC. The reason it exists is because of something called a **DAO Hack**.

DAO

The DAO is a decentralized autonomous organization that is funded on the blockchain. They have a crowdfunding contract on the Ethereum blockchain and were able to raise a large sum of money, and fortunately, there was a weakness to the contract that made it possible to create a sub-DAO and drain funds from it. After a while, there was a vote in the community to make a hard fork at the blockchain, essentially putting all the funds back as they were at the time of the hack. This is an excellent example of the community coming together to solve a problem, but this also leads to a fundamental question. Is it okay to do changes as long as the code did exactly what it was supposed to do, there is a subgroup in the cryptology community that can be called **crypto-anarchists**. They believe that as long as code does exactly what it was supposed to, it's tough luck if you make any mistakes or subject yourself to being hackable. The vote to create a hard fork showed that most of the community disagreed with this. Still, it will be exciting to see what will happen the next time something similar happens to the public Ethereum blockchain or other blockchains for that sake.

From Wikipedia,

A well-known example, intended for venture capital funding, was The DAO, which launched with $150 million in crowdfunding in June 2016, and was immediately hacked and drained of US$50 million in cryptocurrency. This hack was reversed in the following weeks, and the money restored, via a hard fork of the Ethereum blockchain. This bailout was made possible by the Ethereum miners and clients switching to the new fork.

Decentralized Applications

In a traditional application architecture, we could have a service setup that would provide the application in storage, data logic, and user credentials. A client would run an interface of some kind, and these would have a set communication channel. With distributed applications on the blockchain, this can be constructed a bit differently. Shared data is available on the distributed blockchain and exists in many locations, so it doesn't matter if one of the servers goes down.

The same applies to the data logic, where the logic is shared on the blockchain. So as soon as you upload a contract to the chain, it will spread and execute the same regardless of where you run it from. The client in a distributed setup also looks a bit different, since it will be responsible for storing its user credentials and typically store more of the application data. Building applications this way will make your solution very resistant to system failure, and it means that they can fully operate without a centralized system. You can still have functionality in the client for updates towards a centralized system, but you should ensure that your client does not rely on anything centralized. In further sections, while deploying code to Ethereum, we will create smart contracts built in a language called **solidity**. Smart contracts are pieces of code that live on the blockchain and execute commands exactly how they were told to by a shared logic. The contracts make up what will be the data logic for our distributed applications. They can read other contracts, make decisions, send Ether, and they can execute other contracts as well. Contracts will exist and run as long as the network. They will only stop to run if they run out of transactional funding or if they were programmed to self-destruct.

Payment model – Gas

In every distributed system design, it is crucial to have a well-functioning model for protecting the system from unwanted attacks. A general principle should be to make it harder to attack than to defend it. It's hard to do in the physical world. Just consider protecting a building. It's very expensive to put up protection and 24/7 security; however, it's quite inexpensive to build a bomb that will destroy the building. In the digital world, this can be done differently. Just consider using hashing algorithms. They are inexpensive to use, but they're costly to crack. When protecting the blockchain against unwanted behavior, we want to use a payment model that will be fair priced if you use the system as intended, but very expensive if you try to do malicious things to it. This is where the concept of gas comes in.

Gas is the internal pricing for running transactions or contracts in Ethereum. The reason for this is to have a unit that is separated from the current value of Ether. Just think about it like you would for a car. The amount of gas it uses is related to how fast you want it to go, and the price of gas goes up and down, and it's not statically linked to the value of the currency. The amount of gas that a contract or a transaction uses depends on the operations needed to run it. Their price is based on computation, memory, bandwidth, and storage needs, to mention a few. These factors are added together and will make up the gas needed to run the contract or transaction. If you do not have the Ether to cover all the gas requirements to complete running your code, the processing aborts and all intermediate state changes roll back to the pre-transaction snapshot. The gas used up to the point where execution stopped were used after all. So, the Ether balance of your account will be reduced with the price for the gas already spent.

Transactions

The term transaction, when used in Ethereum, needs to refer to the data package that stores a message to be sent from an externally owned account to another account on the blockchain. A transaction contains the receipt of the message, a signature identifying the sender, a value field, which is the amount of `WEI` to transfer from the sender to the recipient, and a gas price value representing the fee the sender is willing to pay for gas. The higher the price you are willing to pay, the higher the miners will rank your work. There's also a start gas value representing the maximum number of computational steps the transaction executed is allowed to take. Think of this as a measurement of the gas tank of a car when filled. This would be the maximum cost, and it will make sure that you are not able to start infinite loops in your code. It is also vital to the miner to get an estimate of how much they can earn by doing the transaction. Since the only way for them to know for sure is after the execution. Since an `out-of-gas` exception is practically a waste of money for a sender, it is always better to overestimate the start gas a little bit than to underestimate. Still, you should be careful of setting a too-high value as well because miners might penalize transactions where there is a big difference between the start gas and the consumed gas. You also have an optional data field that can contain the message sent to a contract. We will look more into this when we start to develop our smart contracts.

Low start gas and gas price

Okay, now let's have a look at the effect of setting the different levels for start gas and gas price. If you set the start gas too low, the transaction will probably not be sent to miners, and you will get an intrinsic gas too low. The same is true if you set a too-low gas price. Miners will ignore the transaction and instead select transactions they can make money on. Setting gas price too low is a bad idea since you will be getting an out-of-gas error, and the transaction is rolled back, but as mentioned, you'll still be charged for what you have used so far. If you set a low gas price, the transaction might be mined slower and put in a later block, depending on the current load of the miner.

High start gas and gas price

If you set a start gas too high, it might result in a delay of getting mined since the miners will think that it will need a lot of resources and must wait for availability. Setting a high gas price will, in most cases, result in your transaction being prioritized and put in a block sooner than other transactions. Each block has a gas limit set to it. If you exceed that with your start gas, the transaction will not be broadcasted to the miners, and you will get an exceeds block gas limit error. If you set a too-high gas price and the sender does not have enough funds available, the transaction is not broadcasted to the miners either.

Medium start gas and gas price

Medium start gas and gas price is generally the ideal level and where you should try to aim.

Conclusion

In this chapter, we started by discussing what and why of Ethereum. We looked at the execution and funding model of Ethereum before we went into distributed applications.

Just remember the core ideas, and you will be fine for developing with Ethereum. Proof of work is the mechanism that works with Bitcoin, the current version of Ethereum, and many other blockchains. Some mining operations also use environmentally unfriendly energy sources. Just to put some aspect to this, the Bitcoin proof of work mining is set to consume the same amount of electricity per year that is consumed by a while midsize European country. In proof of work, a person might take $10,000, use it to buy a mining computer with specialized hardware, and start participating in the network. The mining will then be producing blocks and getting rewarded for the work in the form of cryptocurrency that can be spent. Proof of state attempts to resolve these issues by removing the concept of mining entirely and replacing it with a different mechanism. In proof of stake, one could take the same amount of money and convert it into cryptocurrency straight away. As with proof of work, the more you put in, the more you can expect to get out.

In the next chapter, we will learn about Ethereum with Azure, setting up an Ethereum account with Azure, and setting up a MetaMask account.

Questions

1. What is Ethereum, and what are its denominations?
2. What is the difference between Wei and Ether?
3. What is the value token for Ethereum?
4. What is the average block size in Ethereum?
5. What is a dApp, and why is it different than a regular app?
6. What do you understand by gas and payment model?
7. What happens to the garprice if startgat is set to high?
8. Does gas price determine when a transaction is processed?
9. How is the transaction fee calculated?
10. Where are transactions recorded?

CHAPTER 2
Setting up Ethereum Blockchain on Azure

This chapter will focus on setting up a custom Ethereum blockchain on Azure. The chapter will be less of theory and will focus more on the practical implementation of step by step setting up the Ethereum blockchain on Azure and transferring some Ethers between accounts using MetaMask. The chapter is for the readers who are more into development and have the background of blockchain, Ethereum, and Ether. We have already covered theory in the previous sections of understanding Ethereum and blockchain.

Ethereum on Microsoft Azure

Now let's get into the real fun and start to look at implementing Ethereum. There are many ways to set up and work with Ethereum, and in this section, we will be focusing on working with Ethereum on the Microsoft Azure platform. Azure is a cloud platform from Microsoft, and by using it, we can also quite easily leverage the other aspects of the platform as well. This includes application hosting, storage, identity management, and security, to mention a few. A consortium in the context of Ethereum means collaboration between supporting members of a blockchain with the underlying infrastructure. This could, for example, be a set of organizations that would like to work together and form their own privately shared blockchain. It all starts with the consortium leader. This is the controlling part of the blockchain where you set up the configurations of the chain. This includes the creation of the Genesis block and initial allocations of Ether to the default account.

One important thing to note is that when we are setting up a consortium, this will be a private blockchain that is isolated from the public Ethereum blockchain. Ether from a private blockchain cannot be exchanged directly with Ether from the public blockchain. After the leader is set up, additional members can join in with their infrastructure. We can control who can join our consortium, and we also decide how we will share the available Ether. There are also a lot of ways to set up the infrastructure, but with a default Azure templates, you'll get a baseline infrastructure that would work well in most situations. Let's look at it in detail and see how it works in a running scenario. A user will connect to a publicly available server for applications, and administrative pages run. This must be set up as a separate instance. You should also consider if your client could be set up as a fully distributed application where the client runs on the user device. The application server is set up so that it can make a call into a **virtual private network (VPN)** where it will hit a load balancer that will make a call to one of the many transactional nodes. With the default template, those nodes that are handling the transactions are isolated from the mining nodes, and the mining nodes are not accessible from outside of the virtual private network. This is all you need to create and operate a blockchain, and since all of this is templated in Azure, you don't need to spend time setting this up. It will be done automatically for you. If you decide to add a consortium member as well, they will form their VPN and make a tunnel between VPNs. This also means that if you like, you can host applications on the member networks as well.

Structure

In this chapter, we will discuss the following topics:
- Setting up Azure account
- Setup Ethereum on Azure account
- Setup Metamask and perform transactions.

Objectives

After studying this unit, you should be able to:

- Setup an Ethereum Blockchain on Azure.
- Use Metamask to test the blockchain by transferring Ethers to another account.

Azure account setup

Let's start by setting up an Azure account first. If one does not have a paid Azure account, one could leverage Azure's new account's benefits of giving $200 credits. That means if you are new to Azure and want to play around with its free trial, you'll get $200 credits that you can use to explore Azure. If you are new to Azure and do not have an account, follow the following process, else directly login to your portal.

1. Open the Azure website that is *azure.microsoft.com.*

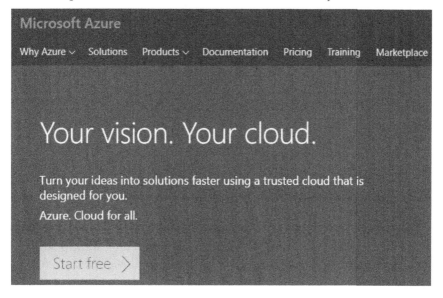

Figure 2.2.1

2. Click on **Start free** to create your free Azure account and get $200 as credits:

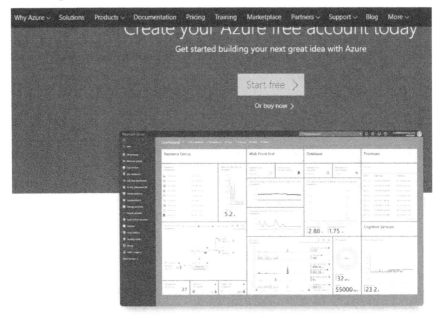

Figure 2.2.2

3. Creating an account and claiming $200 would need your credit/debit card for verification purposes only and will nor deduct any amount from your card. You can play around with this credit and account for 30 days. You'll see the signup page, where you fill all your information and signup step by step. Once signed-up successfully, you'll see the link to the portal, as shown below.

Figure 2.2.3

4. Click on the portal, and you land up on the dashboard and are ready to use/play around with Azure.

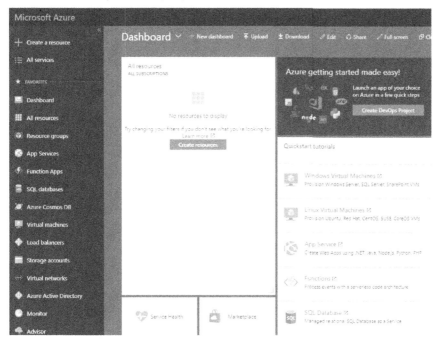

Figure 2.2.4

Ethereum account setup on Azure

1. Once on the dashboard, click on the big + button, that is, **Create a resource** to create a new resource. In the search box, type and enter Ethereum to get all the Ethereum related templates that we would need. Note that you may or may not

see different names or layout on Azure portal for setting up Ethereum as the portal keeps changing time to time:

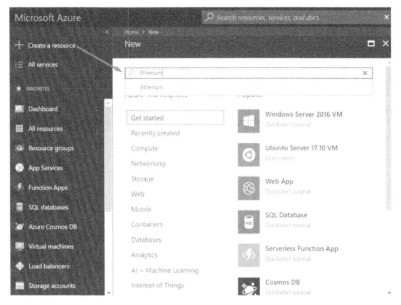

Figure 2.2.5

2. From the list of templates, select **Ethereum Proof-of-Work Consortium.** It is not guaranteed that you see the exact templates, as shown in this section. Since the development is always on for Azure, you may see different names of templates or different templates all together when you are following this implementation.

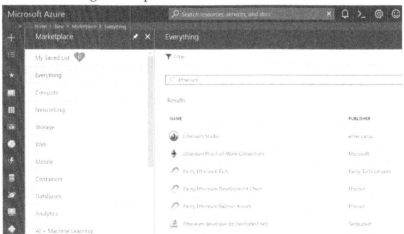

Figure 2.2.6

3. Once clicked on **Ethereum Proof-of-Work Consortium**, leave the deployment model as it is and click on the **Create** button, as shown in the following screenshot:

Figure 2.2.7

Once you click on create, you'll see a page where you need to fill specific details. Following are the step by step creation guidelines.

1. For step **1**, that is, **Basics**, provide the **Resource prefix** to keep the consortium items segregated from other existing resources on your Azure portal. Example, I have given it a name eth, you can have your own or else can use this as well:

Figure 2.2.8

2. Provide the **VM user name** of your choice, as shown in the preceding screenshot. I have used athadmin, though I wanted to use ethadmin; it was a typo from me to use athadmin, which hardly matters as we are developing to learn.

3. You can choose to have an **Authentication type** as **Password** or **SSH public key.** For now, I am using **Password**, make sure you remember the password that you provide here. You can choose to have **Free Trial** as a **Subscription** or your paid account if you have one. Create a resource group, by providing a name so that all your resources in the context of this consortium lie in this resource group. All the items in the resource group share the same permissions, policies, and life cycle. I have provided the name ethrium-blockchain as a **Resource group.** Last, choose a **Location** close to where your application will run. I have chosen **Central India.** Click **OK**.

4. Choose **Deployment regions** in the second step; I have chosen **1** in the number of regions and **Central India** as **First region** for it:

Figure 2.2.9

5. The third step is to choose **Network size and performance** factors. Leave the **Number of mining nodes** to the default value, that is, **2**. I chose **Mining node virtual machine size as 2x Standard D1 v2,** that is, the minimum one and may vary while working on large applications. The choice of virtual machine size and transaction node virtual machine size is directly proportional to size and performance. **Transaction Nodes** could be left to **1**, as shown in the following screenshot. I choose the **Transaction node virtual machine size** as the default one, that is, **1x Standard D1 v2.**

Figure 2.2.10

6. Step **4** is **Ethereum Settings** and is very important. Provide the **Consortium Member Id** as 0 and leave **Network ID** as it is to what is already selected. The network id serves as the name of the Ethereum network that we will set up. It means only the nodes that have the same network id can

pair with each other. You can provide the custom genesis block here, it would be useful if you want to use an existing account for the settings, but for now, we stick to default and proceed to provide **Ethereum account password.** Provide the password, confirm it, and save it somewhere so that you remember. You need to provide the passphrase to generate the private key. Provide the passphrase of your choice and confirm that as well, like done for passwords:

Figure 2.2.11

7. In step **5**, choose the **OMS Workspace Location** as per your nearest location. I choose **Central India** here:

Figure 2.2.12

8. In step **6**, you'll see the summary of what we chose and selected. Review everything, and Click **OK** to go to the **Buy** section.

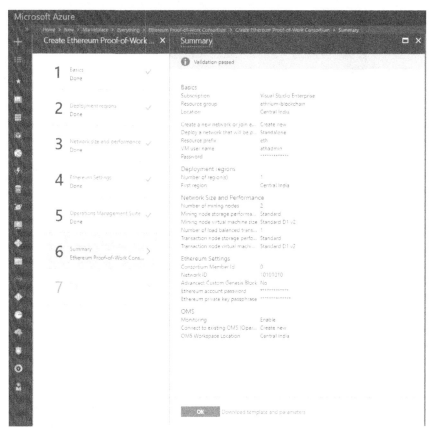

Figure 2.2.13

9. Step **7** is the **Buy** option section, where you read all the terms and conditions before you make a purchase and then click on **Create**:

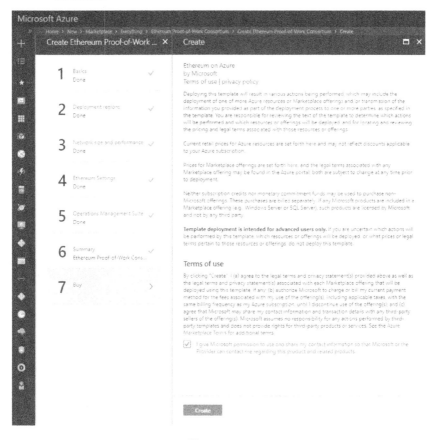

Figure 2.2.14

10. After you click on **Create**, it will take some time to set up and create the resources. It says something like **Submitting deployment for Ethereum Proof-of-Work**...wait for a while, and it would be fine.

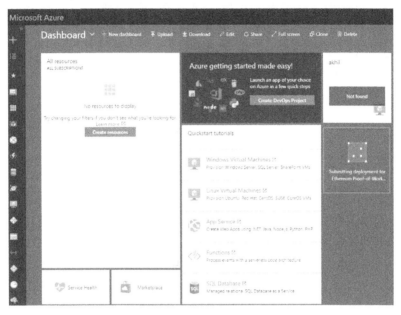

Figure 2.2.15

11. Once the deployment is done, you can navigate to **Resource groups**, as shown in the below screenshot, and choose your newly created resource with the resource group name you provided:

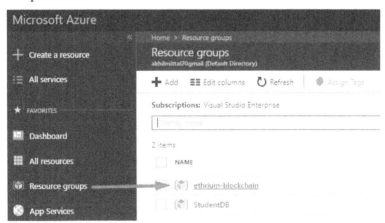

Figure 2.2.16

12. Clicking on the **Resource groups** will land you to all the resources created for the consortium, as shown in the below screenshot. Now click on **Deployments** in the left sidebar to see all the deployments made:

Figure 2.2.17

13. You'll be redirected to the section where you'll see all the deployments made.

Figure 2.2.18

14. Select the first link that is Microsoft-azure-blockchain to find all the information about the newly created blockchain.

Figure 2.2.19

15. You'll get to see the page for sections like **Overview, Outputs, Inputs,** and Template, as shown in the following screenshot:

Figure 2.2.20

16. Choose **Outputs**, and you'll get all the information you need to connect to the chain. Copy the address of **ADMIN-SITE** and open the same in the browser, as shown in the following screenshot:

Figure 2.2.21

17. The admin site would be opened in the browser and would look like below. On this page, you see the information about blockchain. Azure has created a genesis block for us with the default account showing as **My Account Address** on the

page. We see that we also have some Ether balance in our account to get started with our blockchain.

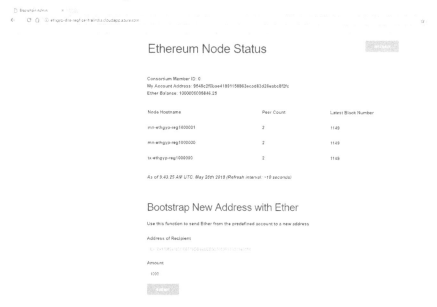

Figure 2.2.22

Half of the job is done, and we have successfully set up an account on Azure for Ethereum blockchain.

Figure 2.2.23

Set up a second account with MetaMask

Following are the steps to set up the second account with MetaMask:

1. To set up the second account to transfer some Ether to it, copy the **ETHEREUM-RPC-ENDPOINT** address, as shown in the following screenshot, from the same location where we copied the **ADMIN-SITE** address on Azure.

Figure 2.2.24

2. Now go to chrome extensions and search for MetaMask in the chrome web store. It is an extension to chrome so that it could be easily added to chrome by clicking on **ADD TO CHROME** button. MetaMask is a useful wallet application for development and testing purposes:

Figure 2.2.25

3. Once added to chrome, you'll see the MetaMask icon in the upper right corner of the chrome browser. This indicates that MetaMask is added to chrome. Click on that icon and click on the **Accept** button after reading the terms and conditions.

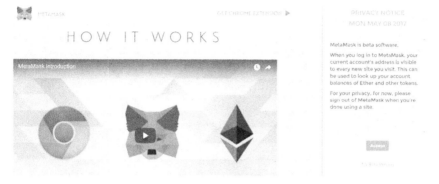

Figure 2.2.26

4. After you click on **Accept**, you'll be redirected to create an account with MetaMask. Provide the password as shown in the following screenshot and click on **CREATE**:

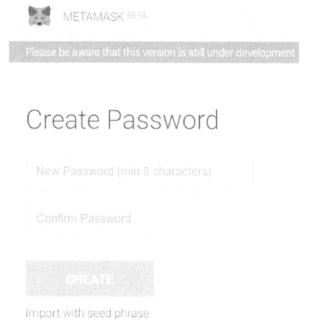

Figure 2.2.27

5. After creating the password, you'll be shown a unique account image that you'll see each time you make a transaction. Click **NEXT**:

Figure 2.2.28

6. On the next page, you'll see the terms and conditions. Read those carefully and click **ACCEPT** if you wish to proceed, as shown in the following screenshot:

Figure 2.2.29

7. After you accept the terms and conditions, you'll be shown the **Secret Backup Phrase**, as shown in the following screenshot used for restoring and backing up your account. Better to save these codes somewhere safe where only you can access. Click on **CLICK HERE TO REVEAL SECRET WORDS** to get the phrase:

Figure 2.2.30

8. On the next page, you need to verify your phrase. So, select the words in the same order as the phrase was initially on that page:

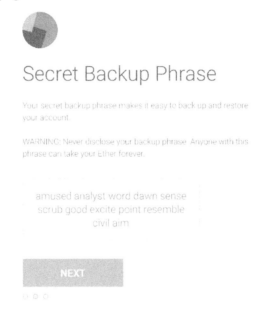

Figure 2.2.31

9. Choose a test network of your choice, as shown in the following screenshot:

Figure 2.2.32

10. Now, under the **Settings** tab, paste the URL that we copied from the Azure portal in the **New RPC URL** text box:

Figure 2.2.33

11. Return to chrome MetaMask extension, and we see our newly created account here now, as shown below. Copy the account address, as shown in the following screenshot:

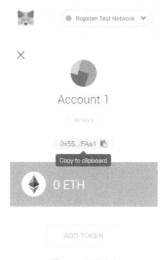

Figure 2.2.34

12.   Go to the admin page we opened in another tab and paste the copied address of MetaMask *Account 1* in the **Address of Recipient** box, as shown in the following screenshot:

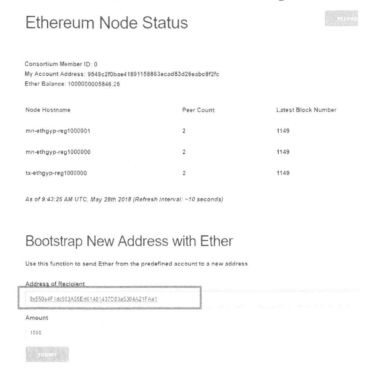

Ethereum Node Status

Consortium Member ID: 0
My Account Address: 9549c2f0bae41891158863ecad83d26eabc8f2fc
Ether Balance: 1000000005846.25

Node Hostname	Peer Count	Latest Block Number
mn-ethgyp-reg1000001	2	1149
mn-ethgyp-reg1000000	2	1149
tx-ethgyp-reg1000000	2	1149

As of 9:43:25 AM UTC, May 28th 2018 (Refresh interval: ~10 seconds)

Bootstrap New Address with Ether

Use this function to send Ether from the predefined account to a new address

Address of Recipient

0x550e4F1dc003A55Ed61481437D83a5304A21FAa1

Amount

1000

SUBMIT

Figure 2.2.35

13.   Add some Ether **Amount** to be sent to the recipient, example, 1000 and click on **SUBMIT**:

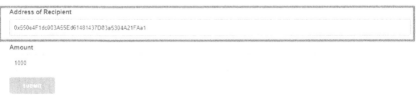

Bootstrap New Address with Ether

Use this function to send Ether from the predefined account to a new address

Address of Recipient

0x550e4F1dc003A55Ed61481437D83a5304A21FAa1

Amount

1000

SUBMIT

Figure 2.2.36

14. Once submitted, you'll see the message **Ether sent!**

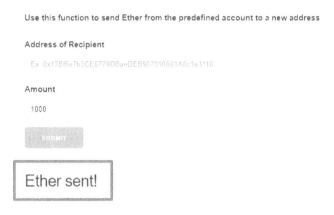

Figure 2.2.37

15. But were they sent? We can quickly check this by again going back to our chrome extension and click on Fox icon. **Congratulations!!** we see the **1000 ETH** transferred to this account now:

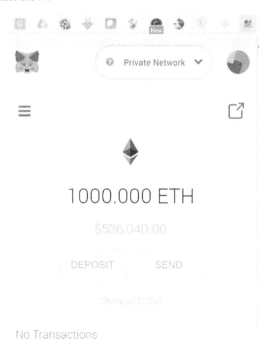

Figure 2.2.38

Hence, we successfully transferred Ethers from one account to another using our Azure blockchain consortium. We can now develop smart contracts for our blockchain. I'll cover smart contracts and other related topics in the upcoming sections.

Conclusion

In this chapter, we learned how to set up an Ethereum blockchain on Azure and use MetaMask to test our blockchain by transferring some Ethers to another account. The next section will focus on smart contracts and how to set up a development environment for writing smart contracts.

Figure 2.2.39

Questions

1. What is Azure?
2. What is the Ethereum proof-of-work consortium?
3. What is a Resource group on Azure?
4. What is MetaMask?
5. What node does MetaMask use?
6. Explain proof-of-work in a simple way.

Section - III
Smart Contracts
Development

In the last section, we learned about setting up Ethereum blockchain on Microsoft Azure using a consortium leader. Time for some development now. Before we move on to smart contracts and their development, it's essential to set up a development environment as a pre-requisite. This section will solely focus on setting up the development environment for smart contract development. In the next section, we'll see what smart contracts are and how we can develop those.

Image credit: https://pixabay.com

Figure 3.0.1

Tools and development environment

We'll use a list of tools to set up our development environment before we proceed with actual development. I'll use a fresh window installation on Microsoft Azure. You can follow the steps to set up a VM on Azure in the last section before we start. We'll install the Chrome browser on the new machine, followed by MetaMask that is the chrome plugin, which will help us in the authentication. Microsoft provides Visual Studio code, that is free, and we can use that as a development IDE for our smart contract's development. We'll install the **NuGet Package Manager (NPM)** and Chocolatey that is also a package manager, to get other tools and packages needed for development. We'll use Git along with NPM and Windows build tools for building/compiling the code. We'll use an in-memory test server known as **Test RPC** to test the application and lastly Truffle. We'll explore more about Truffle when we start development.

CHAPTER 1

Setting up an Environment for Smart Contracts Development

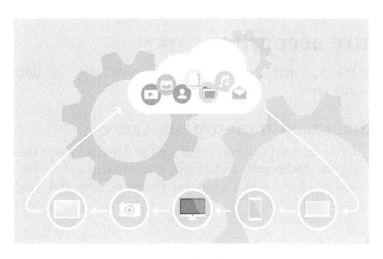

Figure 3.1.1

Azure

Azure is a cloud platform from Microsoft and provides numerous resources in context on cloud computing. One of the resources is a **virtual machine (VM)**, i.e., a fully functional machine of your choice with the choice of your configurations and operating system could be created within seconds with just a few clicks. You can access the machine remotely from anywhere with your secure credentials and do whatever you want, for example, hosting your website, developing applications, creating production or test environment for your software, and many more. Let's see step by step how we can achieve that.

Structure

In this chapter we will discuss the following topics:

- Virtual machine setup on Azure
- Getting the environment ready for smart contract development

Objectives

After studying this unit, you should be able to:

- Setup a development environment for programming smart contracts.

Azure account setup

Follow the steps in the last section to set-up an Azure account if it is not already done.

Virtual machine setup on Azure

1. Once on the dashboard, click on the **Virtual machines** link on the dashboard, and a right panel would open where you see all your VM's. Since we are creating new and we do not

have existing ones, so it would be blank. Click on **Create virtual machine**:

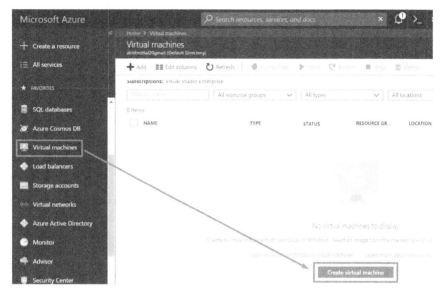

Figure 3.1.2

2. Once you click on **Create virtual machine**, you'll get to see all the operating systems and solution templates that Azure provides to create a machine. You can choose to have Windows or Linux operating system based on requirements, but be careful about costs involved:

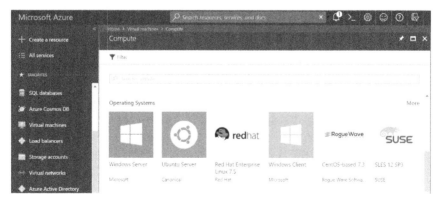

Figure 3.1.3

3. Since this section is for learning how to create a virtual machine, I'll choose the **Windows Client** machine with minimal machine configurations, and one can choose based

on requirements and need. So, choose **Windows Client** as shown in the following screenshot:

Figure 3.1.4

4. You'll get the window of the license agreement and legal terms. Read that carefully and press the **Create** button:

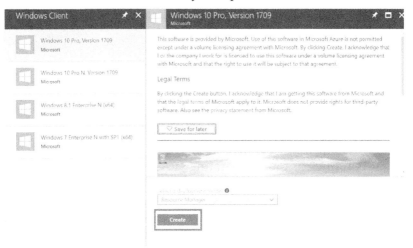

Figure 3.1.5

5. After clicking on **Create**, you'll be asked to fill some basic requirements, as shown in the following screenshot. Give the name as per your choice; for example., I gave it AKHILPC, leave **VM disk type as SSD,** or choose as per your need. Provide a username and password you would need when you connect remotely with the machine. Keep the username and password safe and secure. Choose the subscription, if you have a paid one, choose that else choose the trial subscription that you got. You must provide a **Resource group**. You can create a new or use an existing one. The resource group gives you a logical separation for all your Azure resources. Since

I have an existing resource group created, I am using that. Choose **Location**, click on confirmation checkbox and click **OK**:

Figure 3.1.6

6. Once you click **OK**, you get to see the second section to choose the size of the machine where you see the list of RAMs, Hard disk size, SKU, and zones. Each configuration has a cost associated with it, so choose as per your need and budget. For training/tutorial purposes, I am choosing the first one that has the minimum cost as shown in the following screenshot:

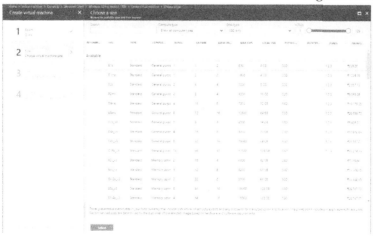

Figure 3.1.7

7. In the third step, you are needed to choose specific settings related to availability, storage, and network. Choose/Provide the settings as per your discretion:

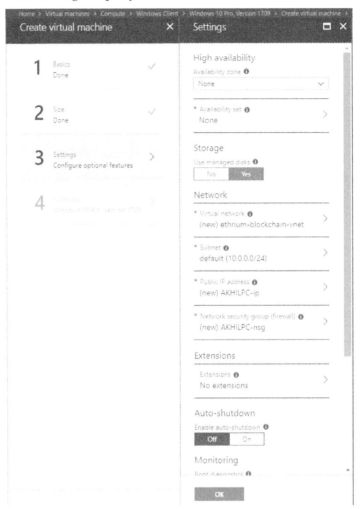

Figure 3.1.8

8. Once you click **OK**, you'll be shown a summary page for all the configuration you choose, cost per hour, and OS. Confirm if everything looks good by clicking on the confirmation

checkbox as shown in the following screenshot, and click on the **Create** button.

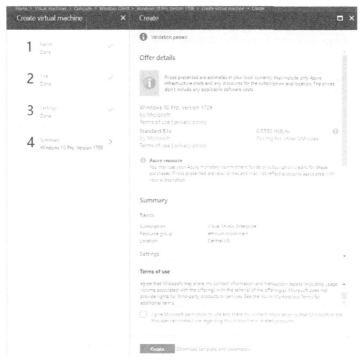

Figure 3.1.9

9. Once you click **Create**, it may take a while to create your VM. It will say **Submitting deployment for**…. Wait till the deployment is complete. For me, it took 5~9 minutes:

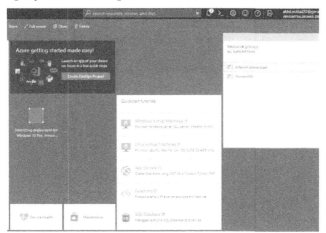

Figure 3.1.10

10. Once the deployment is done, you'll see the section for your deployed VM, where you can choose to **Start, Stop, Restart, Move**, or **Delete** your created VM. Clicking on **Connect** will show you two options in the right panel, that is, **RDP** and SSH. We'll choose to connect via **RDP**, so download the RDP file shown at the right panel. Click on the **Download RDP File** button to get the file. Alternatively, you can directly open RDP connect via an **mstsc** command on your local machine. You get the IP address, as shown in the following screenshot, in the RDP section:

Figure 3.1.11

11. The downloaded RDP file will be located at your local download location. Click on that to configure the RDP connection.

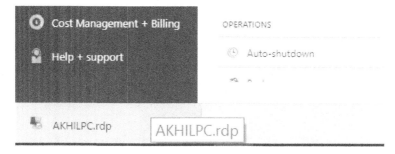

Figure 3.1.12

12. The IP would automatically be filled, just fill the username and password to connect.

Windows Security   ✕

Enter your credentials

These credentials will be used to connect to ▨▨▨▨▨▨▨▨

Akhil Mittal

| Password |

▨▨▨▨▨▨▨▨▨▨▨

☐ Remember me

More choices

| OK | Cancel |

Figure 3.1.13

13. Once the connection is successful, you'll see the Welcome message while window loads and configures for the first-time use. Please wait for a while.

Figure 3.1.14

14. Once Windows loaded, you'll see the desktop as shown below. Now you can choose to do whatever you want with this machine:

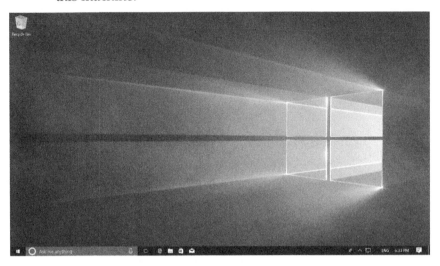

Figure 3.1.15

Note that for the time you use the machine, you'll be charged hourly.

15. In case you do not want to use the machine for some time or stop the machine daily at a defined time, you can do that manually by clicking on the **Virtual machines** option at your Azure dashboard. You'll see your VM. Select your VM and click on **Stop**. You can start whenever you want. Thus, you can save a lot of costs.

Figure 3.1.16

16. Moreover, by clicking on your select VM, you can monitor its hourly/daily usage statistics, as shown in the following screenshot:

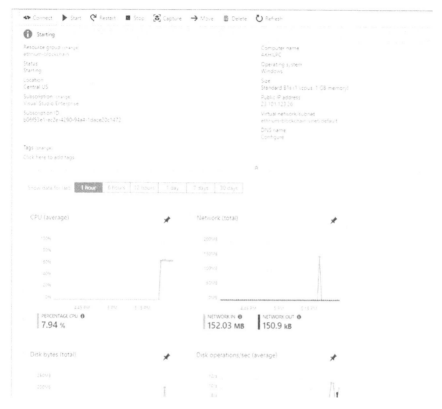

Figure 3.1.17

See how easy it was to set up a VM on Azure with just a few simple clicks. Now you do not have to depend upon any physical machine to do your job.

Step by step installation of tools and packages

As described by me in the earlier section, let's start with step by step installation of other tools and packages:

1. Install Chrome browser - The very first step is to install the Chrome browser. In case you already have Chrome browser, open the browser and refer step 3, else download the Chrome browser:

Figure 3.1.18

2. Read *Google* terms and services and install them on the new machine that is just created.

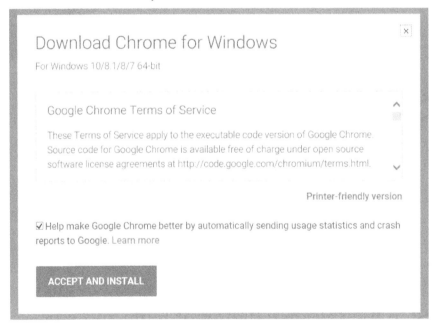

Figure 3.1.19

3. Now we must install MetaMask, that is, a Chrome plugin that will help us in authentication and testing. MetaMask is a tool that helps you to interact with the Ethereum networks in your browser quickly. It uses infura.io. note that Metamask does not support mining and contract deployments.

Download MetaMask from GitHub from the following URL: *https://github.com/MetaMask*. As shown in the following screenshot, choose the `metamask`-extension link shown in **Pinned repositories** and click it:

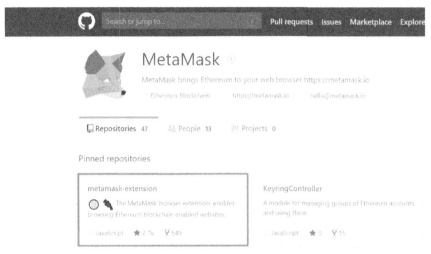

Figure 3.1.20

4. I have chosen the version `4.7.4`; you may see the newest stable version when you try to download that. Download the Chrome plugin by clicking on the link `metamask-chrome-4.7.4.zip`, as shown in the following screenshot:

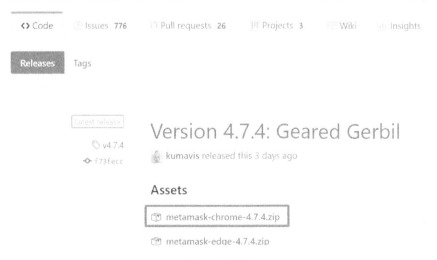

Figure 3.1.21

5. Unzip the downloaded zip file to any location on the Windows:

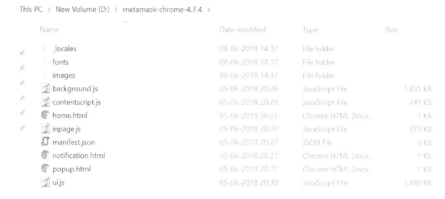

Figure 3.1.22

6. Now open Chrome extension settings by typing following URL in Chrome: *chrome://extensions*. Switch on the **Developer mode**, as shown in the following screenshot, and click on **LOAD UNPACKED**, that is, to load the unzipped downloaded extensions:

Figure 3.1.23

7. Now navigate to the folder where the MetaMask chrome extension was unzipped and choose that root folder, as shown in the following screenshot:

Figure 3.1.24

8. As soon as you click on **OK**, the extension would be loaded in Chrome, and you'll see the MetaMask home page that confirms the extension is now part of the Chrome browser. You'll see a fox icon at the top right of chrome as an extension. Now you can go back to the Chrome extensions page that we opened earlier and disable the **Developer mode** that we enabled while loading the unpacked extension:

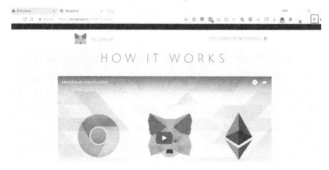

Figure 3.1.25

9. Time to download *Visual Studio Code*, that is, the IDE that helps us in development. VS Code is widely accepted, and a lightweight free IDE provided by Microsoft for development. Navigate to the URL: **https://code.visualstudio.com/**. Download the latest stable build, as shown in the following screenshot:

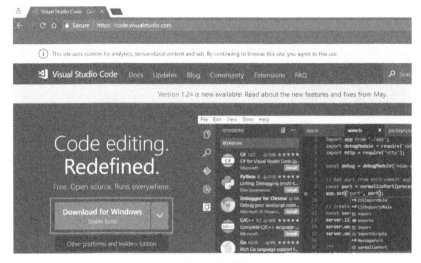

Figure 3.1.26

10. Once the executable is downloaded, click on the same to install that. Read the license agreement and accept it and follow the instructions of the installation setup to get the VS Code to install on your machine:

Figure 3.1.27

11. Now its turn to download NPM. Navigate to the URL - **https://nodejs.org/en** and download the latest released stable version that you see on the window. I am downloading an **8.11.2** LTS version of NPM, as shown in the following screenshot:

Figure 3.1.28

12. Click on the setup once it gets downloaded and follows the steps.

Figure 3.1.29

13. Keep all the settings as default and click on **Next** buttons till the setup is installed successfully:

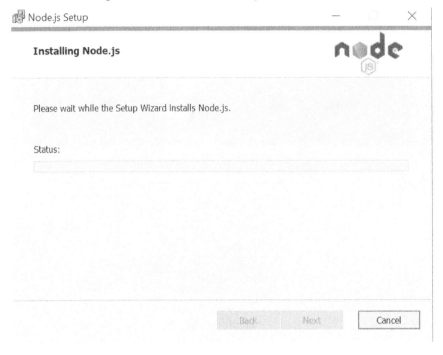

Figure 3.1.30

14. Click on the **Finish** button once the setup is installed:

Figure 3.1.31

15. Now, as discussed earlier in this section that we need one more package manager. Let's install that as well, that is, **Chocolatey**. It could be installed using `PowerShell` commands, and we get the commands/scripts on the URL: **https://chocolatey.org/**. Go to the website and click on the **Install Chocolatey Now** button, as shown in the following screenshot:

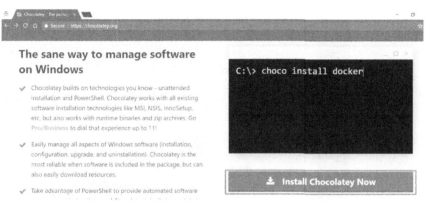

Figure 3.1.32

16. On the page where you land up, scroll down to the section where you see subheading as **Install with PowerShell. exe**. Copy the script, as shown in the red box in the following screenshot. The script would be:

```
Set-ExecutionPolicy Bypass -Scope Process
-Force; iex ((New-Object System.Net.WebClient).
DownloadString('https://chocolatey.org/install.
ps1'))"
```

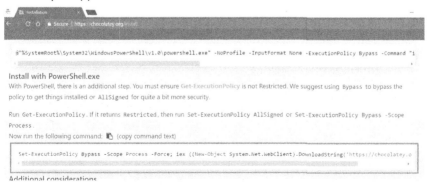

Figure 3.1.33

17. Now open the PowerShell window from your windows start menu as shown below and click on **Run as administrator** to launch the PowerShell command prompt:

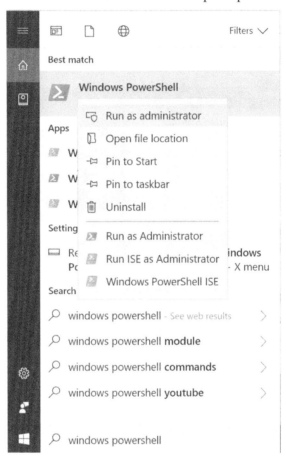

Figure 3.1.34

18. The command prompt would look like, as shown in the following screenshot:

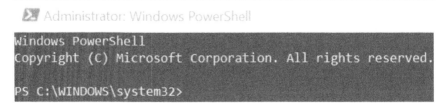

Figure 3.1.35

19. Now paste the copied script to the command prompt and press *Enter*.

Figure 3.1.36

20. Once Chocolatey commands and NuGet packages are in place, we'll install GitHub client using the install command of Chocolatey; this installs other useful tools that would be used during development.

    So, type command: choco install git -params "/ GitAndUnixToolsOnPath" in the command prompt as shown in the following screenshot and press *Enter*.

Figure 3.1.37

21. The installer on command prompt will ask to run the script for allowing Global Configuration. You can type *Y* for yes and press *Enter* to allow it.

```
Do you want to run the script?([Y]es/[N]o/[P]rint): Y

@{Inno Setup CodeFile: Path Option=CmdTools; PSPath=Microsoft.PowerShell.Core\Regist
psoft\Windows\CurrentVersion\Uninstall\Git_is1; PSParentPath=Microsoft.PowerShell.Co
WARE\Microsoft\Windows\CurrentVersion\Uninstall; PSChildName=Git_is1; PSDrive=HKLM;
\Registry}
Using Git LFS
Installing 64-bit git.install...
git.install has been installed.
git.install installed to 'C:\Program Files\Git'
  git.install can be automatically uninstalled.
Environment Vars (like PATH) have changed. Close/reopen your shell to
 see the changes (or in powershell/cmd.exe just type `refreshenv`).
 The install of git.install was successful.
  Software installed to 'C:\Program Files\Git\'

git v2.17.1.2 [Approved]
git package files install completed. Performing other installation steps.
 The install of git was successful.
  Software install location not explicitly set, could be in package or
  default install location if installer.

chocolatey installed 3/3 packages.
 See the log for details (C:\ProgramData\chocolatey\logs\chocolatey.log).
PS C:\WINDOWS\system32>
```

Figure 3.1.38

22. Now close and re-open the power shell window to ensure everything is installed correctly.

Figure 3.1.39

23. Let's now execute some commands as follows,

- Turn of all calls secure feature in Git: git config –system http.sslverify false

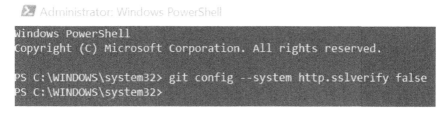

Figure 3.1.40

- Install node addon build tool via NPM: npm install -g node-gyp

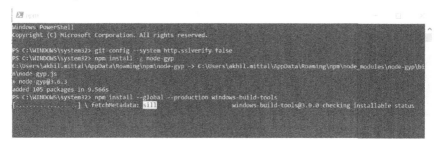

Figure 3.1.41

- Install windows build tools: npm install --global --production windows-build-tools

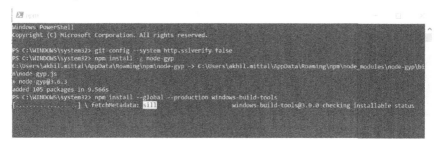

Figure 3.1.42

- Installing windows build tools will take some time, so be patient and, in the meanwhile, have something to eat if you like ☺.

Figure 3.1.43

24. Install Test RPC that is the local Ethereum server for testing our solution: `npm install -g ethereumjs-testrpc`

Figure 3.1.44

25. Lastly, we install the Truffle toolset: `npm install -g truffle`

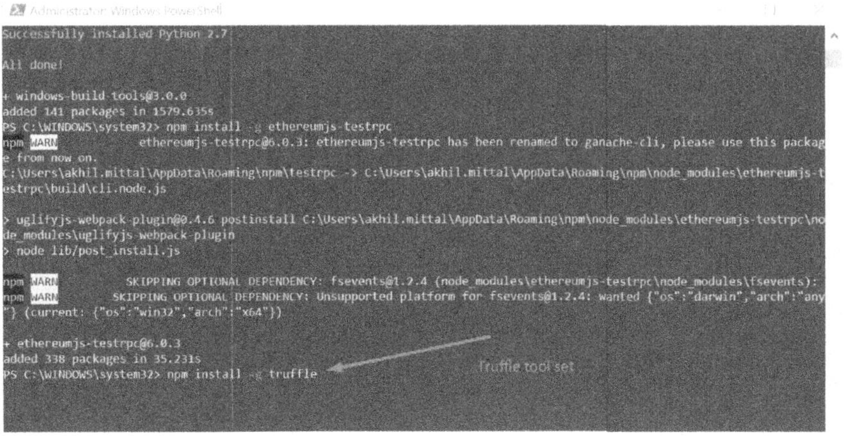

Figure 3.1.45

Now we are good to start our development as our tools and software are well in place, and our development machine on Azure is up and running. Yes, it was a lot of work to set up the environment and tools, but don't worry, it would be fun to develop and learn these new tools and technologies.

Conclusion

In this chapter, we learned how to set up the development environment to start development. We came across various packages like NPM and Chocolatey that helped us to install more tools. We installed the VS Code, MetaMask, which will help us to provide a coding environment. In the next chapter, we'll focus on smart contracts and development. *Cheers!*

Questions

1. What is Chocolatey?
2. What are the build tools used to compile smart contracts?
3. How do test RPC and truffle work?
4. What is MetaMask?
5. What node does MetaMask use?
6. What are the limitations of MetaMask?

CHAPTER 2
Programming Smart Contracts

Making a smart contract is, in many ways, quite like what you might be used to already. You start by writing the code in a supported language. That will be different depending on the blockchain implementation you are working towards. In this chapter, we will be using a language called **Solidity**, which is supported by Ethereum, and it's currently gaining support in the Bitcoin blockchain as well. Another current option would be writing Serpent code, which also has some community support for Ethereum. After writing the code, it must be compiled to byte code. There are several compilers available. There are even online compilers that will get you started quickly. In this section, we will use a framework for working with smart contracts that are called **Truffle**. Truffle has a built-in compiler that is very easy to get started with. When a compile is done successfully, we upload our contract and wait for it to be mined. After a contract is successfully mined, we can start interacting with it. In most cases, you would create a user interface towards the contract, but you can interact directly with it through HTTP POST operations.

In the last chapter on smart contracts development, we learned about setting up the development environment before we start coding or developing our first smart contract. We installed the necessary packages and tools that would be needed for development. In the section, we'll explore Solidity and develop our first smart contract of `Hello World`.

Image credit: https://pixabay.com

Figure 3.2.1

Structure

In this chapter we will discuss the following topics:

- Smart contracts
- Byte code
- EVM
- Smart contracts and solidity
- Truffle and test RPC
- Smart contract development
- Smart contract deployment
- Test smart contract.

Objectives

After studying this unit, you should be able to:

- Develop your basic smart contract.
- Learn the basics of solidity.
- Test smart contract.
- Deploy smart contracts.

Building blocks - Smart contracts

Smart contracts are the software programs that run automatically as soon as any amount specified in the contract has been transferred to Ether. Therefore, no (manual) verification of a payment receipt is required because the transfer starts directly as specified in the program consideration.

The entire blockchain stores each transaction - on all devices connected to the network. The decentralized concept of blockchain permanently checks the integrity of the entire database.

Byte code

The smart contracts are usually written in the solidity, a high-level programming language specially developed for Ethereum. Those are then translated in bytecode and run on the `Ethereum Virtual Machine (EVM).` A virtual machine encapsulates a client environment away from the host environment, that is, the other applications on a computer.

This is very similar to a programming language like *Java*, where the code gets converted to JVM byte code. The Ethereum runtime environment only understands and can execute the bytecode.

This design gives developers the liberty to make use of other programming languages to create smart contracts. One of it is Vyper, which is very much like Python and compiles down to EVM bytecode.

EVM

The EVM is a simple but powerful, turing complete 256 bit VM that allows anyone to execute arbitrary EVM byte code. EVM plays a significant role in the consensus engine of Ethereum and is part of the Ethereum protocol as well. It allows anyone to execute arbitrary code in a trust-less environment in which the outcome of execution can be guaranteed and is entirely deterministic.

Smart contracts and solidit

Developing smart contracts is nothing but writing code in the supported language of the blockchain implementation for which we need to develop a smart contract. For example, Ethereum supports the language named **Solidity**. The code after been written needs to be compiled to bytecode. There are many compilers available for it, and few are available online as well. In this section, we will use Solidity to write code and a framework named *Truffle* that we installed in the last section. Truffle provides us with an inbuilt compiler to compile the smart contract. After successful compilation, the smart contract needs to be uploaded/deployed and mined. Once it is successfully mined, one can start interacting with it. The interaction could be done via user interfaces for the contracts or straightaway via HTTP POST method operations. Solidity provides us the flexibility to write code following object-oriented principles. It is the language that is very much like the style of *JavaScript*.

Figure 3.2.2

A developer coming from the background of an object-oriented programming language can quickly grasp Solidity and its syntax. Solidity supports both standard and multiple inheritances, and its data types and coding structs are very much like any other object-oriented language. Example bool is the keyword to support Boolean data types that can hold either true or false as a value. Strings, as usual, are used with double quotes but have minimal string manipulation capability that we find in other languages like *C#*, *JavaScript*, or *Java*. Solidity has both signed, and unsigned integers are having a range of 8 bit to 256 bits. One of the essential types that Solidity uses is the address type. It is used to store addresses used in Ethereum for an account or a smart contract. Solidity has support for access modifiers like public, private, internal, or external. Access modifiers help to provide an abstraction to the code and more control on who can access the code from where. If it needs to be accessed from everywhere, the Public is used. If the code needs to be accessed within a contract, then we use Private. Internal means that a contract and its deriving contracts, that is, child types, could use the code, that is, methods and properties. Using external only allows contract methods and properties to be used externally, and none child types could access those as was in internal.

A contract in Solidity is defined by a contract keyword and the name of our choice to the contract. This is very much like writing a class in any programming language. A contract, after been defined, can have methods and variables. One of the essential things to remember is that we can have multiple return types in methods in Solidity.

Truffle and test RPC

Truffle is a toolset framework for development, testing, and asset pipeline for Ethereum development. Truffle includes tooling to compile and build your solution. It enables a framework for automated testing, and it makes deployment of our contract very simple with the support of configurable deployment locations. Another great thing about Truffle is that we can use it in console mode as well to interact directly with our deployed contracts. This is quite cool, and I'll show you how it works shortly. When working with smart contracts, we must know that our contracts work as expected before we unleash them to the world because we don't have a feasible option for doing a take two. Uploading to a blockchain test environment on the net will take some time. It is, therefore, very time-saving to use a local test blockchain instead. Test RPC is an easy-to-use, in-memory blockchain that is great for testing your contracts while developing. Not having to wait for an external blockchain will speed up your development in the early phases. Test RPC implements EthereumJS, which is the same set of instructions that you'll find in the real Ethereum blockchain. Another great thing about Test RPC is that it will automatically create 10 throwaway test accounts for you with the connected private keys.

Developing a smart contract

Let's start developing our first smart contract of `hello world`. We'll start with executing test RPC and create a project with the help of Truffle and then create our `hello world` contract.

1. Create a new folder in your windows with the name `helloworld`:

Figure 3.2.3

2. Once done with folder creation, open a new instance of PowerShell in administrator mode, as shown in the following screenshot:

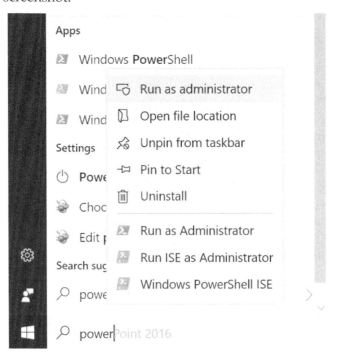

Figure 3.2.4

3. Now, using the cd command, go to the folder we just created, that is, `helloworld`, as shown in the following screenshot:

```
Administrator: Windows PowerShell

Windows PowerShell
Copyright (C) Microsoft Corporation. All rights reserved.

PS C:\WINDOWS\system32> cd D:\Articles\BlockChain\3\SourceCode
PS D:\Articles\BlockChain\3\SourceCode> cd helloworld
PS D:\Articles\BlockChain\3\SourceCode\helloworld>
```

Figure 3.2.5

4. Now, we'll use truffle to kick-start our solution. This will get the framework and simple project created for us in the `helloworld` directory that will help us to start quickly. So, type command truffle `init` and press *Enter* in the power shell window:

```
Administrator: Windows PowerShell

Windows PowerShell
Copyright (C) Microsoft Corporation. All rights reserved.

PS C:\WINDOWS\system32> cd D:\Articles\BlockChain\3\SourceCode
PS D:\Articles\BlockChain\3\SourceCode> cd helloworld
PS D:\Articles\BlockChain\3\SourceCode\helloworld> truffle init  ←
Downloading...
Unpacking...
Setting up...
Unbox successful. Sweet!

Commands:

  Compile:        truffle compile
  Migrate:        truffle migrate
  Test contracts: truffle test
PS D:\Articles\BlockChain\3\SourceCode\helloworld> ▂
```

Figure 3.2.6

5. As you see in the preceding screenshot, the command runs, downloads necessary packages and sets up or development environment. You can go back to the `helloworld` folder to check the folders and files created for our development environment:

Figure 3.2.7

6. Now you can launch VS Code and open the folder for our source code, or you can follow a more straightforward method by just typing code . in the power shell console window. This will open up the folder for us in our IDE, that is, visual studio code.

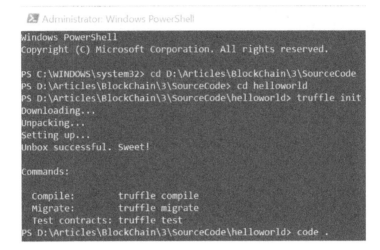

Figure 3.2.8

7. Once VS Code is launched, you can see the files and folders loaded in the solution. We see that it has automatically created some test contracts for us. Let's leave it as it is for now and move to the next step.

Figure 3.2.9

8. Time to create a new contract. Right-click on **contracts** and add a **New File.**

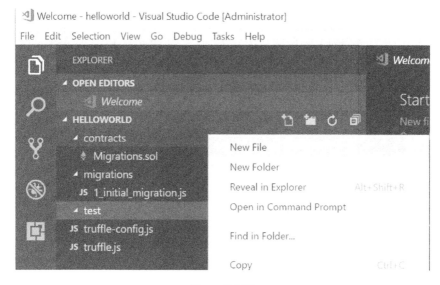

Figure 3.2.10

9. Add a new file with the name of your choice. In my case, I have given it a name helloworld.sol, as shown in the following screenshot:

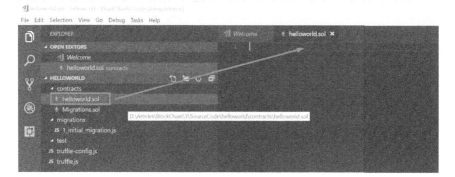

Figure 3.2.11

10. Let's write some code now. Before we proceed to write our method, we will set pragma, as shown in the following screenshot (first line of code) to 0.4.22, which means it works with any version of solidity about 0.4.22. In this way, we would be confident that our code works exactly as expected with the set version.

11. Next, define a contract with the name `helloworld` followed with opening and curly braces just like we do while defining a class, and inside those brackets will be our methods, properties, and variables. Define a function called `PrintHelloWorld ()` that returns a string in the way as shown in the following image and return a hard-coded string saying `Hello World !`.

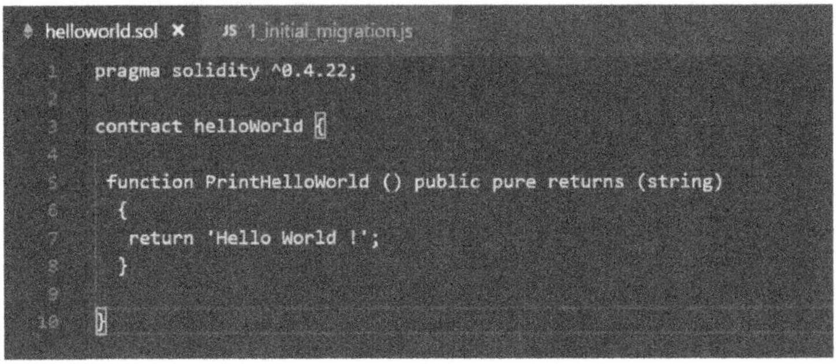

```
pragma solidity ^0.4.22;

contract helloWorld {

function PrintHelloWorld () public pure returns (string)
  {
    return 'Hello World !';
  }

}
```

Figure 3.2.12

Our code looks like as follows,

```
pragma solidity ^0.4.22;

contract helloWorld {

 function PrintHelloWorld () public pure returns
(string)

  {

   return "Hello World !";

  }

}
```

Now, save the file by using *Ctrl + S*. The next step is to deploy the contract.

Deploying smart contract

1. Under the migrations folder, we find the file that tells truffle that which files need to be deployed to the blockchain. In that file, create a deployer for `helloworld` as well by creating a variable named `HelloWorld` requiring the file `helloworld`.

sol and in the `module.exports` write `deployer.`
`deploy(HelloWorld)`, as shown in the following screenshot:

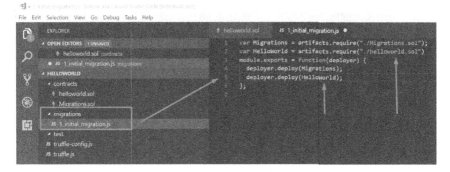

Figure 3.2.13

2. The code looks like as follows:

```
var Migrations = artifacts.require("./Migrations.
sol");

var HelloWorld = artifacts.require("./helloworld.
sol");

module.exports = function(deployer) {
    deployer.deploy(Migrations);
    deployer.deploy(HelloWorld);
};
```

3. Now we need to run the Test RPC server. To do that, open
a fresh new instance of Windows PowerShell and leave the
already opened instance as it is. Type the command `testrpc`,
as shown in the following screenshot, to start the server. We
could see as described by me earlier, as soon as it starts, it
creates test accounts and private keys for us, and the very
first account is used as a default account. Some of the features

may need access from admin to get started. So, in case a window pops up asking for access, please allow:

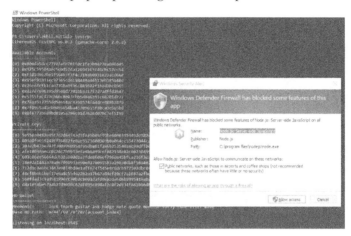

Figure 3.2.14

4. We can see that by default, the server runs at the port 8545. Now since our server is up and running, leave this window open as it is and go back to the prior PowerShell window that we were working on.

Figure 3.2.15

5. It's time to compile our solution now. Use the command truffle compile to compile the solution. Once compiled, as shown in the following screenshot, it will write artifacts to the build\contracts folder.

```
PS D:\Articles\BlockChain\3\SourceCode\helloworld> truffle compile
Compiling .\contracts\helloworld.sol...
Writing artifacts to .\build\contracts

PS D:\Articles\BlockChain\3\SourceCode\helloworld>
```

Figure 3.2.16

6. Now we are good to deploy the contract as it is successfully compiled. We can do the deployment via truffle migrate command, as shown in the following screenshot. Type the command press *Enter*.

Figure 3.2.17

Yes, we get an error:

Image credit: https://pixabay.com

Figure 3.2.18

7. The error says that it could not determine the current network. So, there is some preparation we need to do to get that working. You can skip *steps 5 to 7* if you do not get an error, as it may have configured on your version. But for the one who gets this error, please follow *steps 5 to 7* as well as described below.

8. Go back to VS Code where the solution is opened, and we see a file there named `truffle.js` that should contain the server configurations:

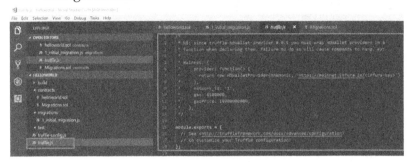

Figure 3.2.19

9. By default, everything in that file is commented out, and we can define our custom configurations. So, replace the complete text in that file with the following code:

```
module.exports = {
  networks: {
    development: {
      host: "localhost",
      port: 8545,
      network_id: "*" // Match any network id
    }
  }
};
```

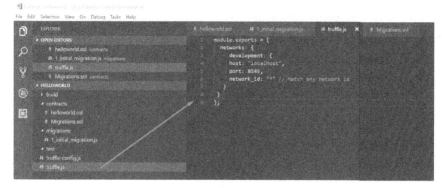

Figure 3.2.20

10. Now add a new migrations file under migrations node as shown in the following screenshot and call it `2_deploy_contracts.js` and move the deploy code from `1_initial_migration.js` to this newly created file:

Figure 3.2.21

11. So, the file contains the code as below.

```
var HelloWorld = artifacts.require("./helloworld.sol");

module.exports = function(deployer) {

  deployer.deploy(HelloWorld);

};
```

12. Now again, go to the PowerShell window where we got an error and again compile the code by typing the command truffle compile and press *Enter*. Once you press *Enter*, the code will again be compiled for the latest changes we made in VS Code. Now again, run the command truffle migrate for deployment.

Figure 3.2.22

This time our migrations run fine as they find the current running server. See the above image as it successfully deploys our contract. We can also see the address it got while uploading.

13. Now, you can go ahead to create a user interface to test the contract we just deployed; alternatively, Truffle also provides a mechanism to interact with the contracts. We can do this via truffle console. To start the truffle in console mode, run

the command `truffle console,` as shown in the following screenshot:

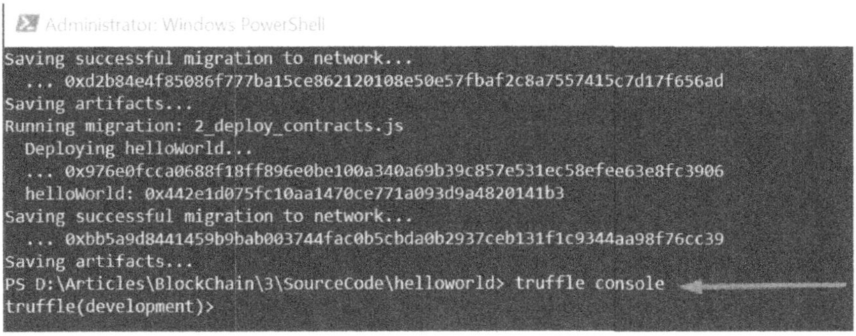

Figure 3.2.23

This opens a console listener for Truffle. In this mode, we can directly write *JavaScript* code for our contract. Let's do it step by step.

Test smart contract

In the truffle console mode, define a variable named `helloW` or any of your choices with the var keyword. And press *Enter*. We'll try to access our contract with this variable. After pressing *Enter*, we get undefined, and that is obvious because the variable is still not defined with any content. Since the communication with contracts should be async, we write an asyn code to access the contract now. Since in our code, the contract was referenced using the deployed keyword, so we'll also access it via `helloWorld.deployed();` after that, a then keyword is used to create an async method that maps our deployed contract with the variable that we created earlier, i.e., `helloW`. The command would be `helloworld.deployed().`

then(function(deployed){helloW=deployed}); See the following screenshot with all the commands to understand in detail.

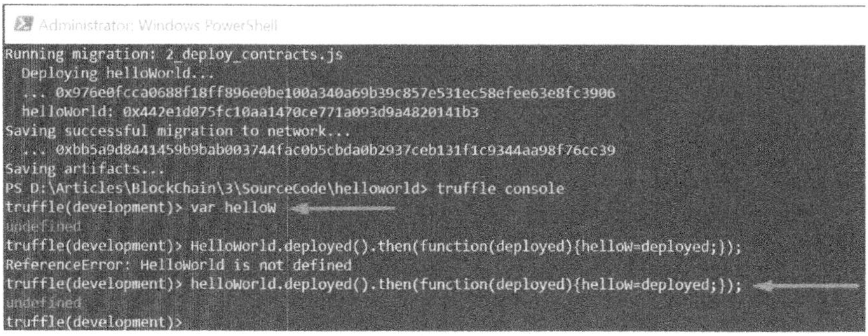

Figure 3.2.24

Now, access and test the contract with the variable we mapped it to in our last step. Use the method `call()` to the `helloworld` contract method to invoke the contract as `helloW.PrintHelloWorld.call()` as shown in following screenshot:

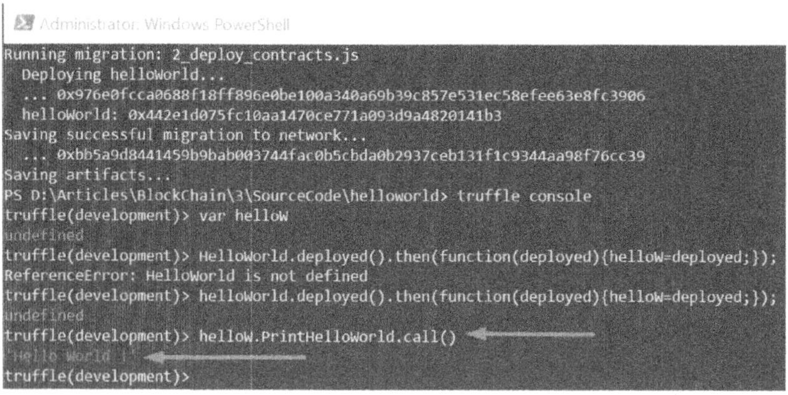

Figure 3.2.25

Here we get the string that we were returning from that method and so our method and contract are tested running on internal private Blockchain.

Was it fun to implement and test our smart contract?

Conclusion

In this chapter, we learned about smart contracts, and the language used to develop smart contracts on Ethereum, Truffle, and Test

RPC. This section serves as a primer to those who are beginners in blockchain development and new to Ethereum and smart contracts. This section gives a foundation on how to start and proceed with smart contract development. I hope you enjoyed creating your smart contract, deploying, and testing it.

Happy Coding!

Figure 3.2.26

Questions

1. What is a smart contract? Which language is used to develop a smart contract?

2. What is byte code?

3. How do you compile the smart contract?

4. What is the very first thing you must specify in a solidity file?

5. What is a smart contract mining?

6. What is the use of Test RPC in smart contract development?

7. Can smart contracts be trusted?

8. Are there standards for smart contracts?

9. Is the execution of smart contracts free?

10. What happens if the execution of a smart contract costs more than the specified gas?

Section - IV
Blockchain in Real World

Let's talk a bit more about what is the need of blockchain, and what more offerings can blockchain provide.

CHAPTER 1
Blockchain-Offerings and Usages

Structure

In this chapter we will discuss the following topics:

- Need, usages, and offerings of blockchain.
- Impact of blockchain technology in education.

Objectives

After studying this unit, you should be able to:

- Understand the real-time applications of blockchain
- Understand how blockchain is impacting/influencing day to day life.
- Understand what all places blockchain technology can contribute or is contributing to?

Need, usages, and offerings

The vital question your company should ask is, do we need a blockchain? There's a simple list of questions that you can ask to help determine this. First, do you need a shared public database between multiple parties? If we're using a public blockchain, do you need the data on this blockchain to be accessible by anyone? If you're using a private blockchain, do you need for this data to be shared between several known parties or companies? If the answer is no, then a blockchain might not be the best technology for you to use. The next question to ask is if multiple parties need to share the data, do any of these parties have conflicting incentives, or are they not trusted? One of the primary purposes of a blockchain is to enable trust between multiple parties. So, if there is a level of distrust between the other parties and they have conflicting incentives, then a blockchain is an excellent solution to look at.

Otherwise, a blockchain may not be needed, and you can use a database instead. The next question you should ask is, are the other parties able to play by the same rules? By this, we mean, will you be able to get them to use the same rules to govern the transactions added onto the blockchain and the same rules to verify the transactions? If the answer is no and you don't think you can get all the parties to play by the same rules, which is easier said than done, then a blockchain isn't going to be an excellent solution to use.

The next question is, do you need an immutable log of all actions to be recorded? Blockchains work best with transactional data like financial transactions or insurance claim settlements, for example. For transactions like this, it makes sense to log them in a long chain of related data items. If this isn't something you intend to do, then a blockchain is the wrong solution. If you answered yes to all of those questions, then you've probably determined that a blockchain will be useful to your organization. At this point, you need to determine whether you are happy to use a public blockchain where everyone is participating in the network and can access and verify your data, or whether you want to use a private blockchain, which is more limited to a consortium of companies.

There are many emerging blockchain implementations, but if you look at the current major ones, we have, of course, the Bitcoin blockchain as the biggest one. Ethereum from Consensus and Microsoft is getting quite a bit of traction from the makers of non-financial applications. It is also the implementation that we will be using later in this course. IMB blockchain on Bluemix is also an alternative for those who want to create their blockchain.

Usages for blockchain

Now that you know the most critical technical aspects of blockchain, let's discuss some of the current usages for it and why it can be such a real `game-changer`. As mentioned, many times in this book, the current most broad use of the blockchain is with digital currencies like Bitcoin. Because anonymous transactions can be trusted just as much as they can with any bank, this opens up a wide range of new ways to deal with global transactions. Let me give you a real-life example. A good friend of mine is a refugee from one of the most horrific wars in modern history. He managed to escape, but his wife is still left in the country. Making sure that she has the financial means to survive is crucial.

Before blockchain, the only option to provide her with money from the other side of the world was by using money- transferring agency. These are very costly, and they take a rather large cut of my friend's limited funds when transferring. Furthermore, transactions can take many days to complete. And lastly, they require that she shows up personally to collect the money, which is not very safe. With blockchain, however, there is no need for a large transferring agency, and there are apps where you can transfer money almost instantly with transfer costs that are only a small fraction. Believe it or not, but even in war-torn countries, you will be able to find the Internet and transfer the money directly to a mobile device. We only see the very beginning of how these kinds of solutions will change the world in ways; we cannot even grasp yet. A small revolution that has been going on for sometimes is called the **Internet of things (IoT)**. This is where small smart devices use the Internet without human intervention. Right now, there are many more devices using the Internet than humans. With using blockchain, these devices can suddenly do trustworthy transactions securely.

An example of this is that your washing machine could order detergent for you when it notices that it's getting empty. The product lifecycle is another where you store all the information on workflow or product in the blockchain. It could, for example, follow the lifespan of a car from the factory through the seller to the customer into the workshop and, lastly, to the recycling plant.

Certifications are also a significant area of use. Certification bodies could issue certifications to products or organizations in a tamper-free and fully transparent way. The secure sharing of data is another example. Given the nature of blockchain, you could insert encrypted information into it and make sure that only those you allow can access your information. This could be used, for example, with medical information or medical devices in a secure manner. Suddenly, all hospitals in the world could have instant access to your medical folder when needed, and you would be able to track everyone that has tried to access your information. There are now devices that will measure the sound of your veins when blood rushes through them. This sound is unique for everyone, and it does not change during your lifespan. Just imagine using these sounds are your private key to the data on the blockchain. The making and selling of virtual and digital products have been snowballing for a long time now. With blockchain, you can market, sell, and even control your digital products like books, courses like these, and music, to mention a few. A musician can upload her music to a blockchain and try different models of buying the product. She could, for example, have one price for listening, one for making a ringtone, and another one with a commercial license for using it in an app. All can be done without a significant organization taking the threat of the royalties. Just try to imagine all the possibilities that lay in front of us now.

More usages

Blockchains have many different use cases when it comes to storing data. Let's take a look at a few of them. The first one and most public use for a blockchain, as we've already discussed, is digital currencies like Bitcoin. We've already touched on this, but this is the most common use at the moment for blockchain technology. Another new use for a blockchain is electronic voting. At the moment, when you vote for a president or prime minister, you have to go to a polling station, put a piece of paper into a box, and then trust a team of people to count the votes correctly. Even in this day and age, this system can be easily rigged. Using a blockchain, votes for candidates can be registered anonymously from your mobile and personal device. Then many nodes on a network will all begin verifying and validating the vote so that nobody can tamper with the process. Another exciting use is that of protecting intellectual property. Digital information can be copied and redistributed with ease on the Internet. This makes retaining and proving copyright hard. A blockchain can be used to store digital signatures of people's work, along with a timestamp and a blockchain, which means there is immutable proof of ownership for that work. Of course, if we have the timestamp baked into the digital signature, we can prove when that piece of work, whether written or an image, was placed onto the blockchain. Next, we have a use case around **anti-money laundering (AML)** and know your customer compliance practices for financial services companies. Currently, financial companies must perform a labor-intensive and expensive process for each new customer. Know your customer costs can be slashed dramatically though with cross-company client verification where once a person has been identified, the results and all the scans of identifying documents, like passports, can be placed onto the blockchain and digitally signed. This makes it easier for that person to be verified in the future, as their details are already baked onto the blockchain. By having this data on the blockchain, it can be utilized by many financial companies because they each are contributing to the identity data, as well as verifying its integrity. Another use of blockchain is tracking items through a supply chain. As an example, you could have a journey of food from farmer to shop being tracked so that as you purchase food items, you can see where it was originated from and that it has not been tampered with in its journey. Finally, the recording of land registry deeds or any other type of public or official documents. Using accessible public ledgers like a blockchain can be useful for any kind of record-keeping. These types of documents can be victims of fraud, as well as expensive to administer. As properties are bought and sold, the details of their sale and transfer of ownership can be permanently written onto a blockchain. This is by no means an exhaustive list of potential applications for blockchains, but it should give you an idea of some potential use cases.

Impact of blockchain technology in education

Blockchain's capabilities are not limited to Bitcoin and financial transactions; instead, it has a broad scope that could be leveraged in our education industry as well. Blockchain can have its implementation in educational institutions like universities, in the publishing industry, or a group of educational institutions as well. It could be used to gather education data, qualifications, and credits more securely and transparently. The following are five areas where blockchain technology would be an excellent choice.

Education institutions

Universities and other educational institutions that offer a project-based education or training can leverage the blockchain technology to generate a tamper-proof certificate for their students. An encrypted certification with two-factor authentications could be kept in the blockchain database generating a unique decentralized number that could be used by the authorities for authenticity. This will prevent anyone from producing a fake or non-authentic certificate. A few international education institutions have already adopted this methodology to ensure certificate authenticity and security.

A global database for qualifications

Not limited to just storing a certificate securely but using blockchain technology, a global (international) database could be created where an individual does not have to store their paper degrees and qualification certificates, which are very prone to lose or tampering. A blockchain-based platform could be established to store all the qualification information which could be used by authorities like Visa officers to check the authenticity of an individual if he is traveling cross-border or migrating, a company's management to check the authenticity of their employee or if they are hiring a new employee, and education institutions to check the background and authenticity of produced qualifications by an individual.

Learning platforms

Individuals in corporate offices or students in educational institutions can have a platform where they can seek online training or sessions with their peers/bosses or teachers, respectively. An independent learning platform could be established between a trainer and a trainee and the terms and conditions for training like projects, tasks, fees, duration of training could be readily agreed upon between both the parties and could be stored as smart contracts for a transparent and secure execution thereby eliminating the concept middleman. He can make money in this way.

Corporate learning

There is a need for a more secure and transparent system for the employees and the companies in which they work for corporate training. Tracking the achievement of an employee or on the overall company's capabilities of providing extensive training is a challenge and hard to measure. The legacy learning management systems and technologies are outdated now. Blockchain technology in this space can play a crucial role in keeping track of all the training done and employees' achievements more securely and transparently where an employee can also leverage this record to showcase to his new employer.

Secure payments

Students can use this platform for paying their tuition/course fees to educational institutions via cryptocurrency. The *Cumbria Institute for Leadership and Sustainability* had already announced an option in *2014* where students can pay their fees in Bitcoins. Accepting payments via Bitcoins does not have to depend upon a significant infrastructure but is the more secure mode of payment. Moreover, international students, or students located globally, can find this an effortless way to pay their fees and do not have to depend upon third parties who can make money via charging fees or conversion rates to students or educational institutions.

Conclusion

This was a detailed theoretical chapter focussing on blockchain's needs, usages, and impact. We saw that the impact of blockchain is broad, and the usages vary from education to security to medical usages as well. It is all about understanding it, adopting it, and implementing it.

Questions

1. Why is blockchain a trusted approach?
2. What are a few popular platforms developing blockchain applications?
3. How can blockchain impact education technology?

Made in the USA
Las Vegas, NV
08 December 2023

82320288R00075